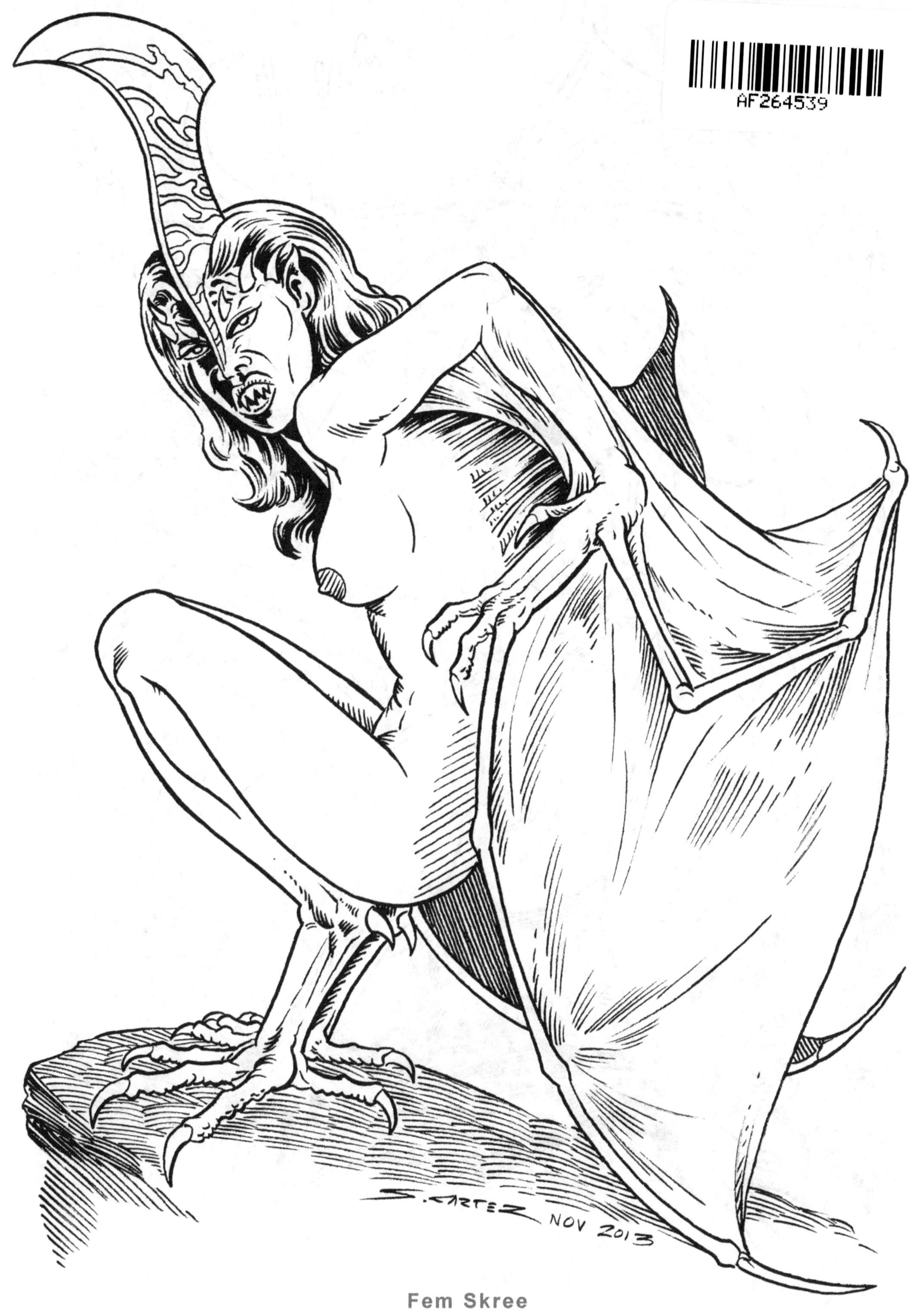

Fem Skree

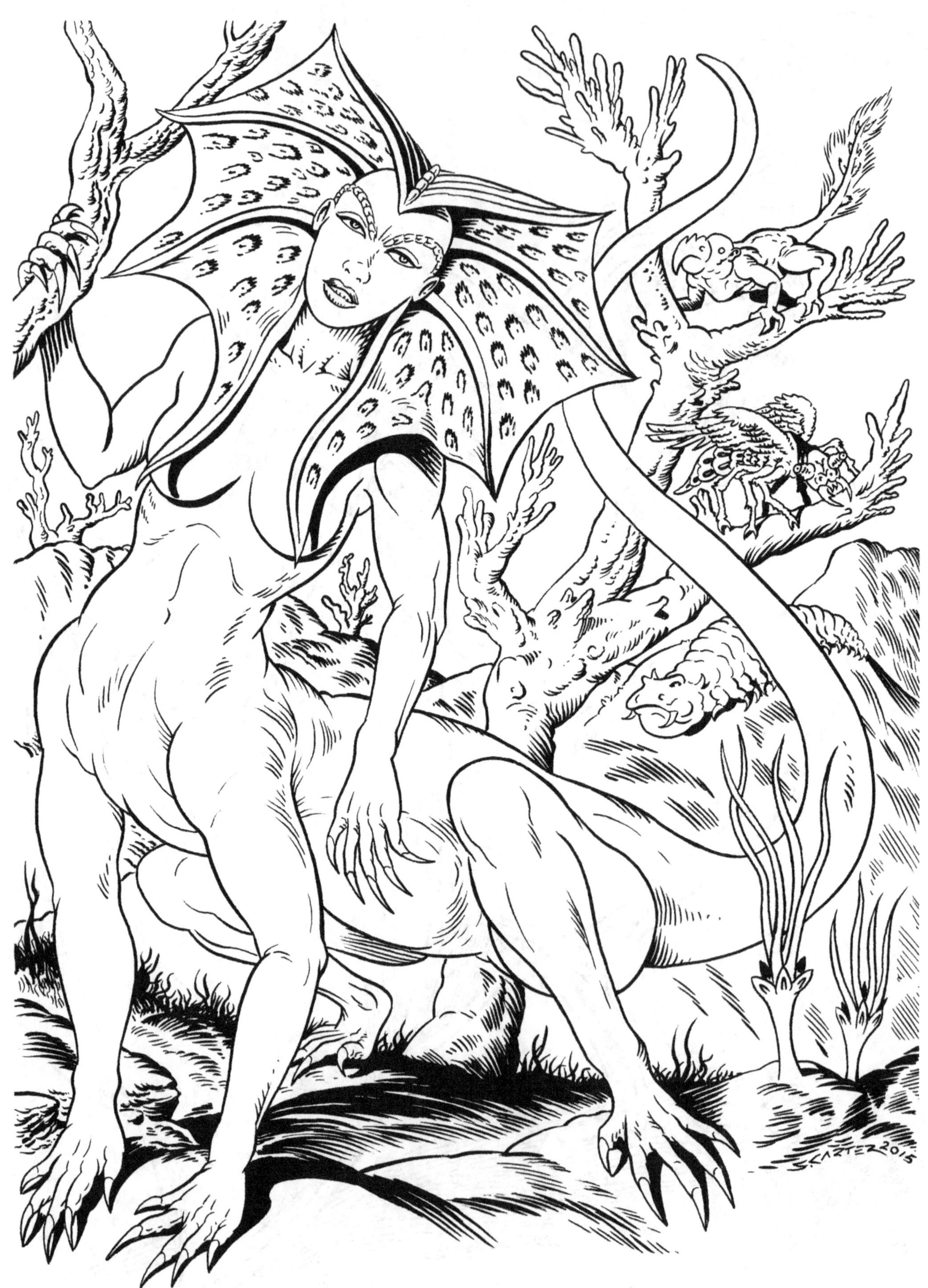

The Skinx

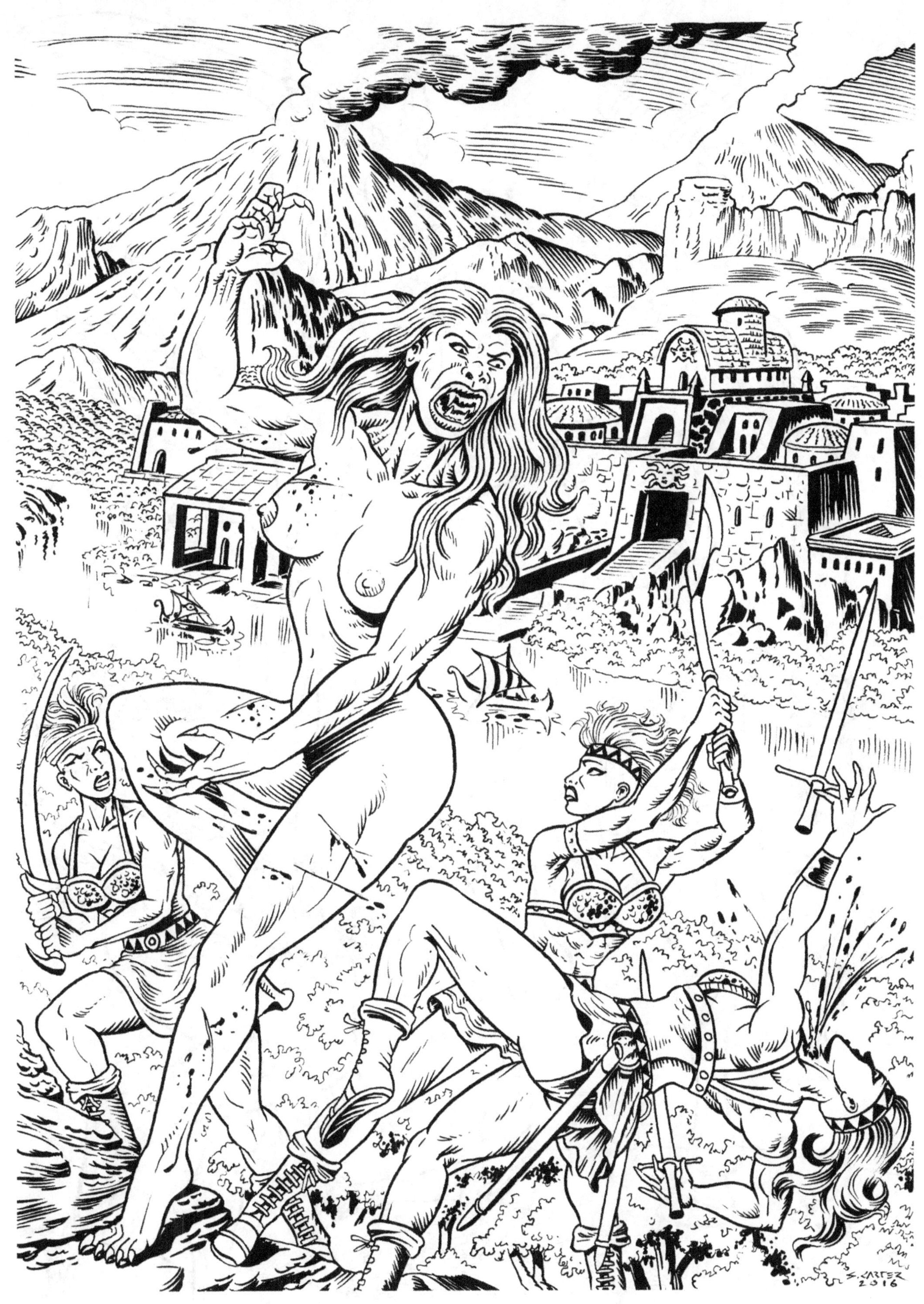

Brutess Battles the Amazon Avengers

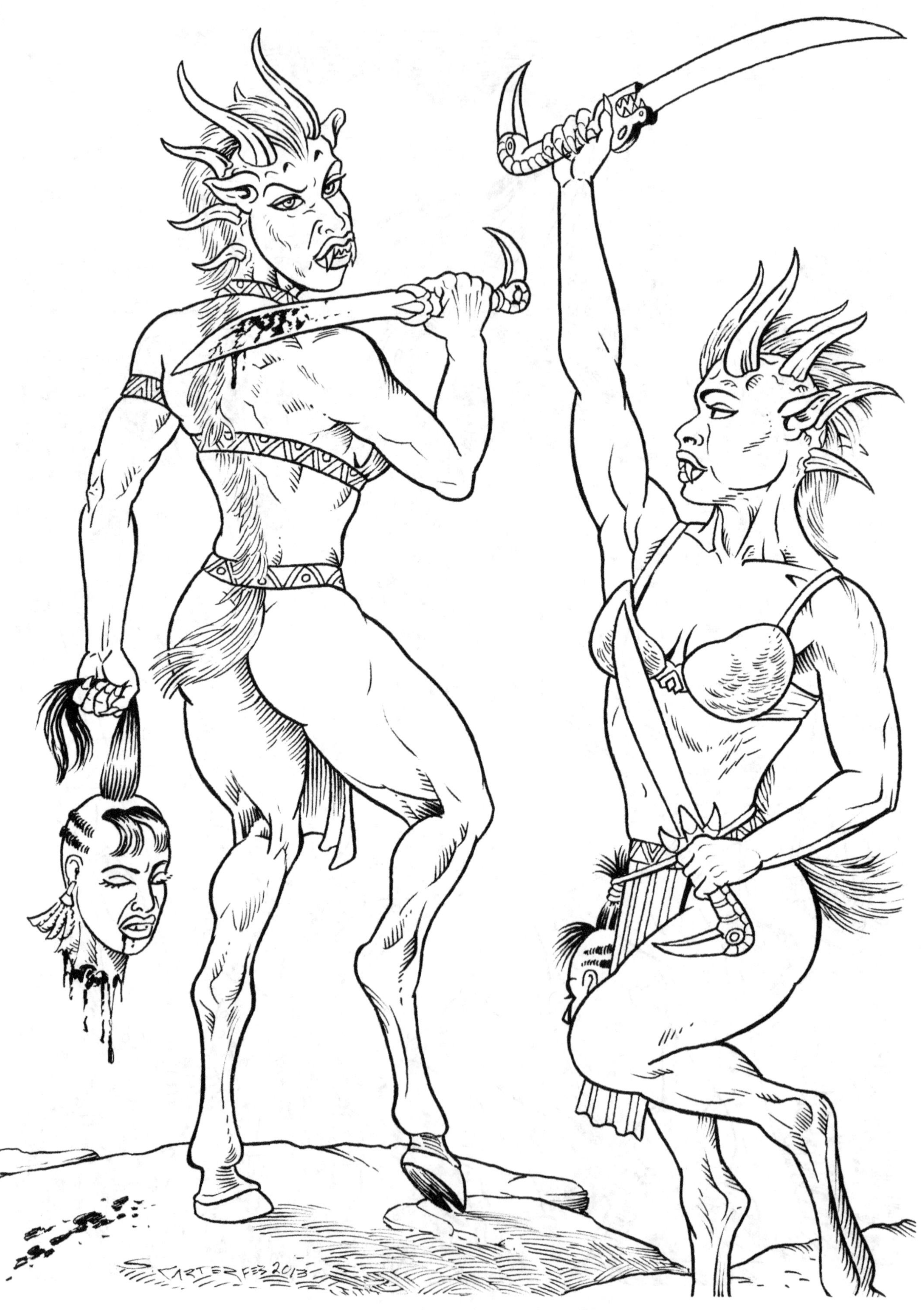

Jubilant Trophy Hunters

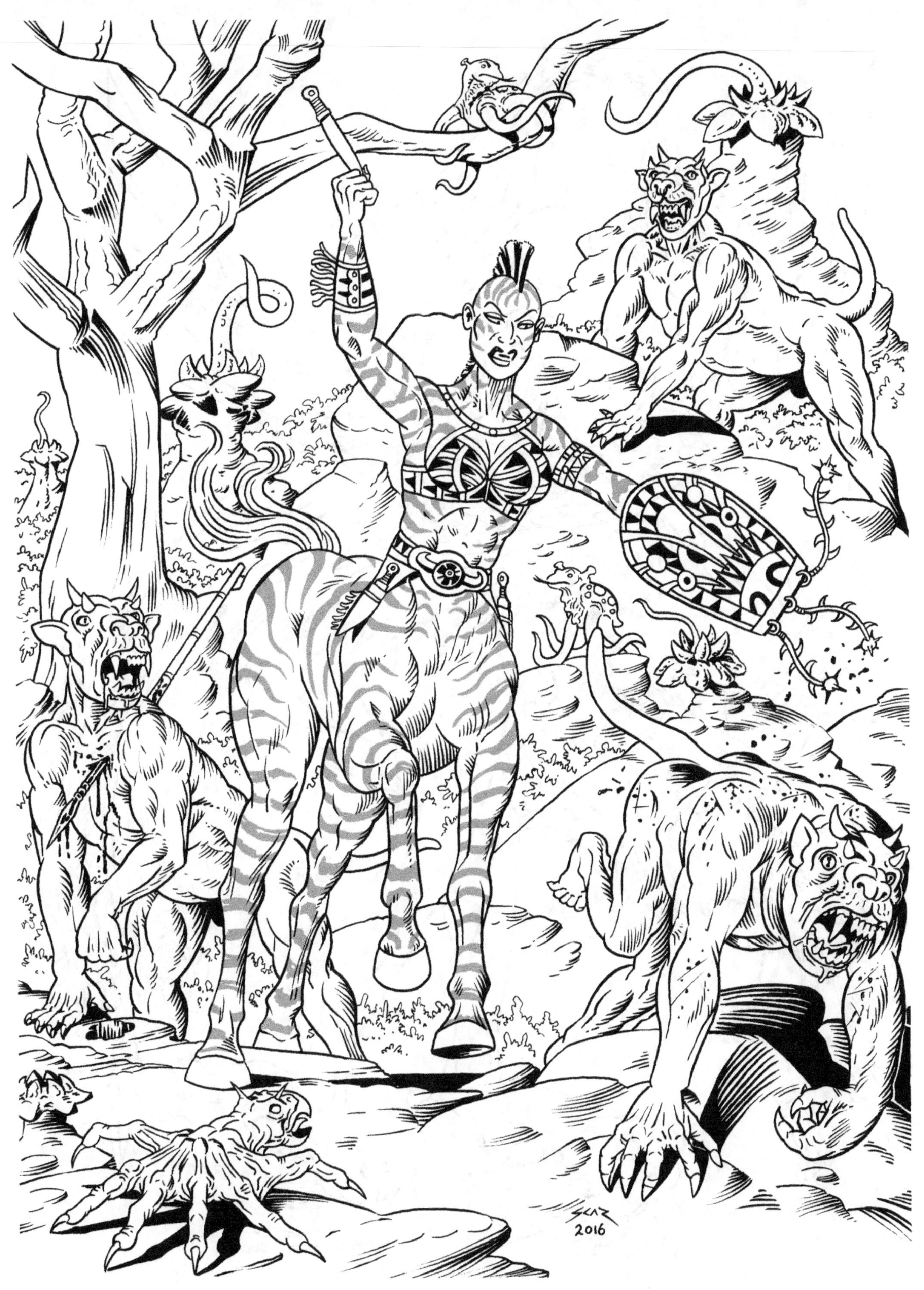

Amazebra Attacking Bush Devils

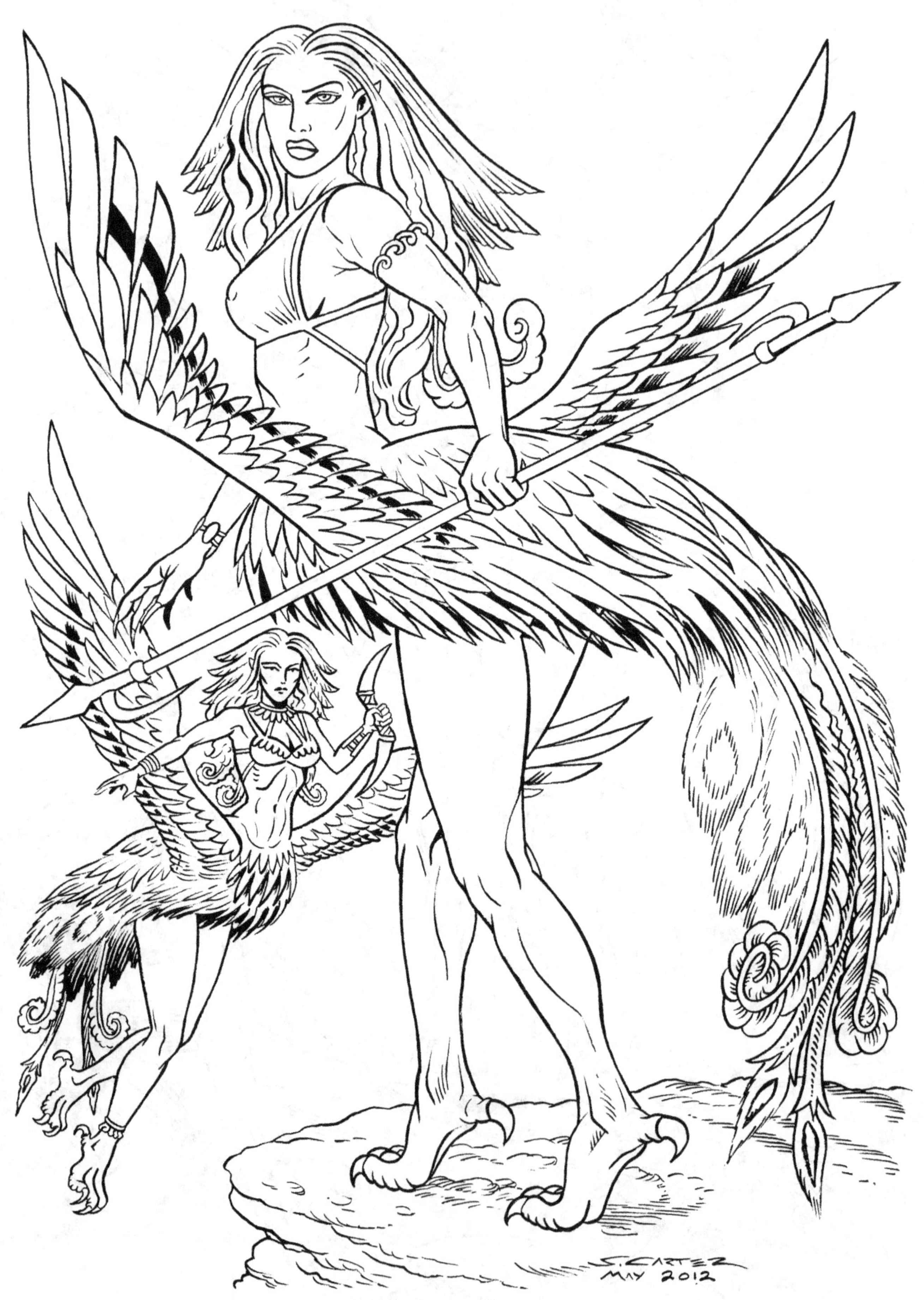

Slash Winged Ullu

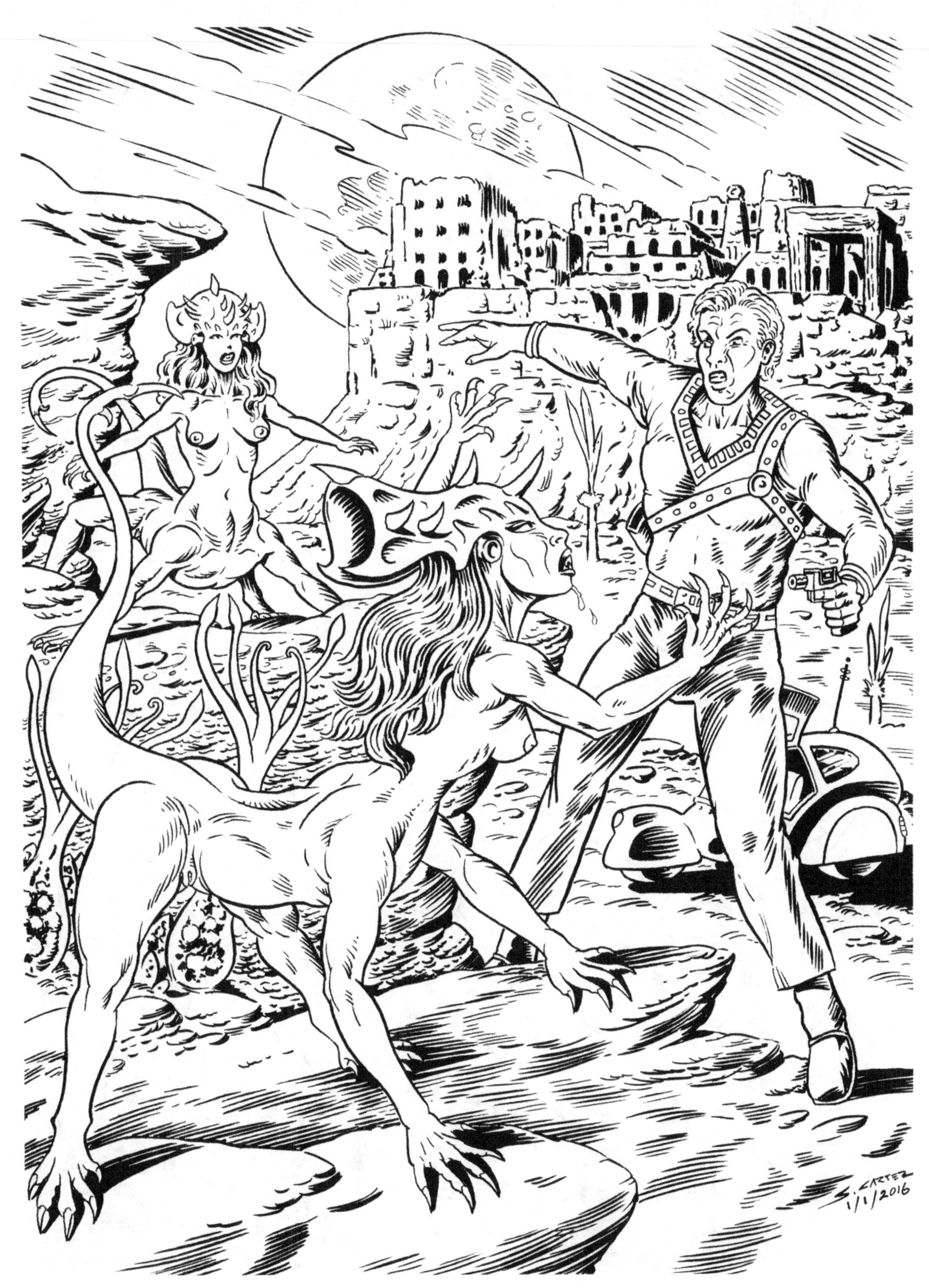

Dangerous Encounter

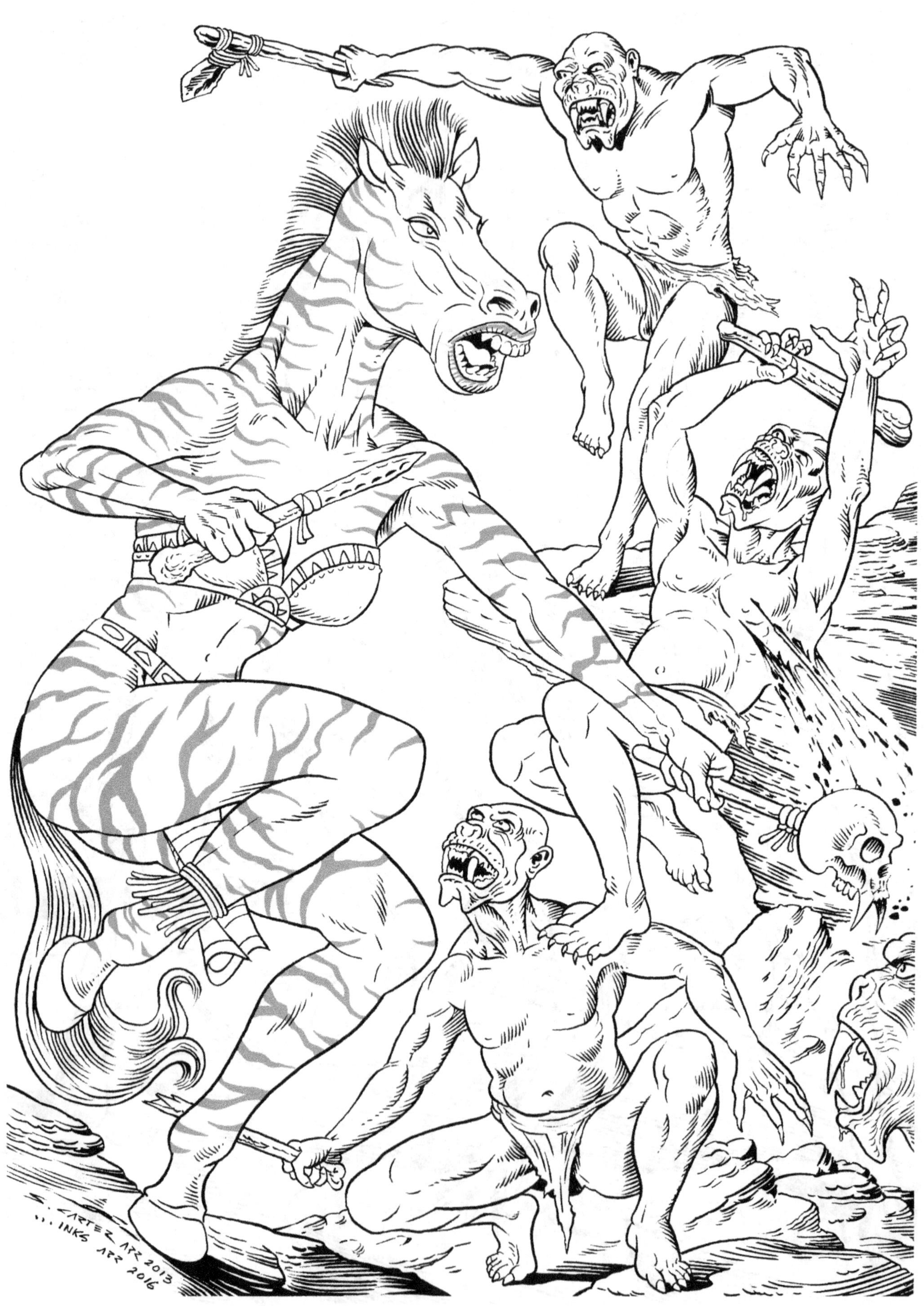

Zebrazon Ambushed

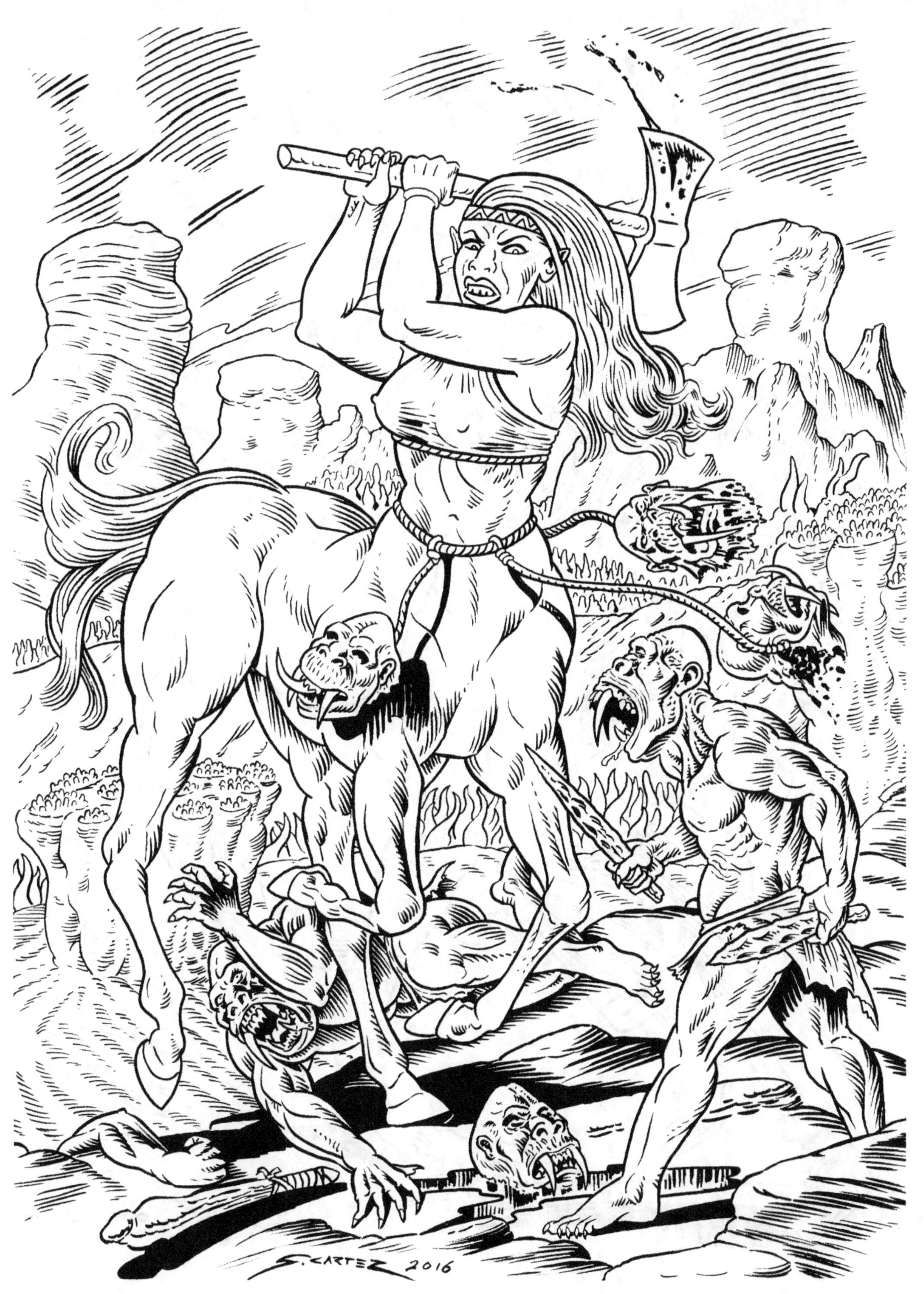

Head Hunting Empussa

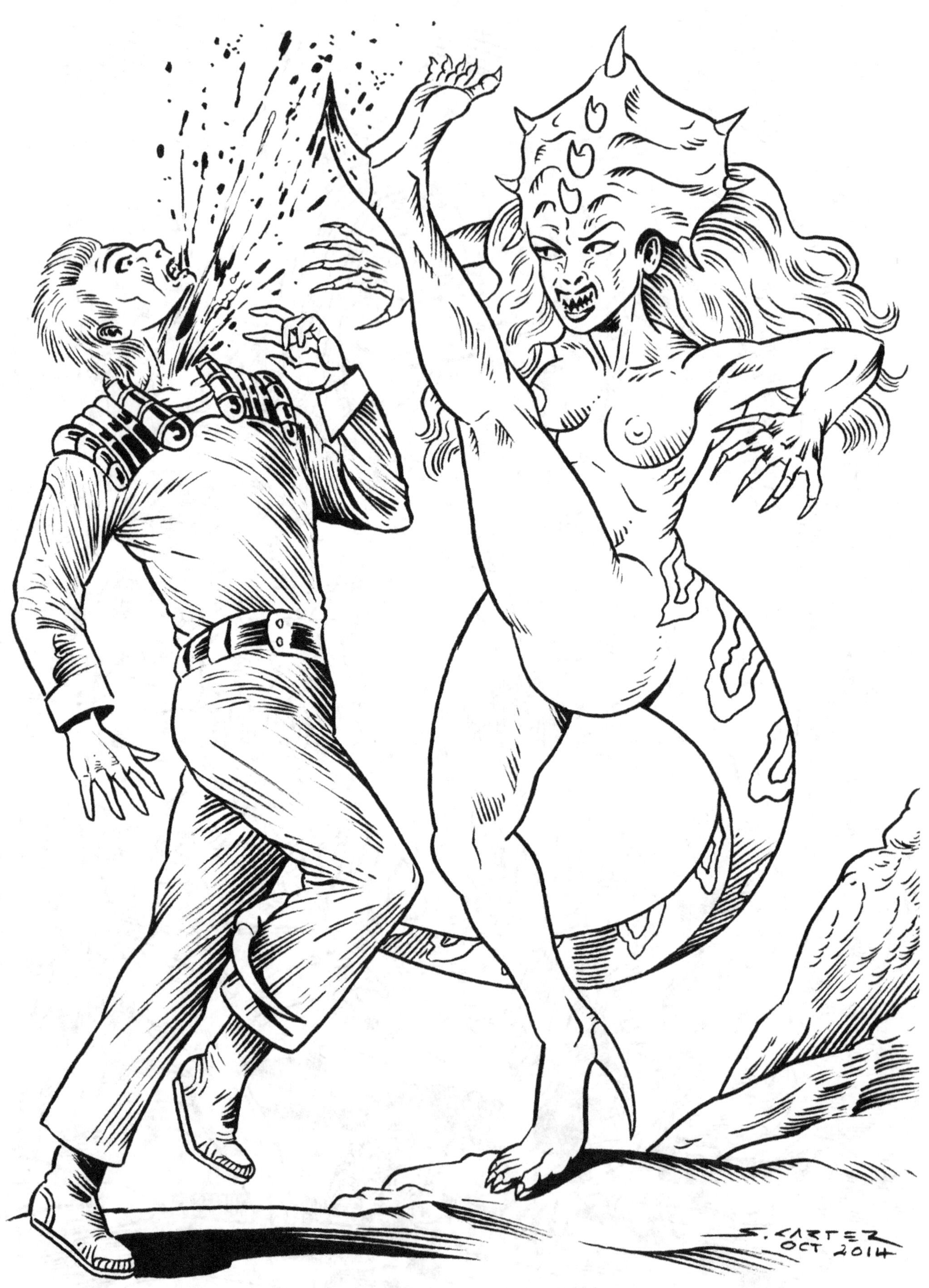

Stiletto Death Blow

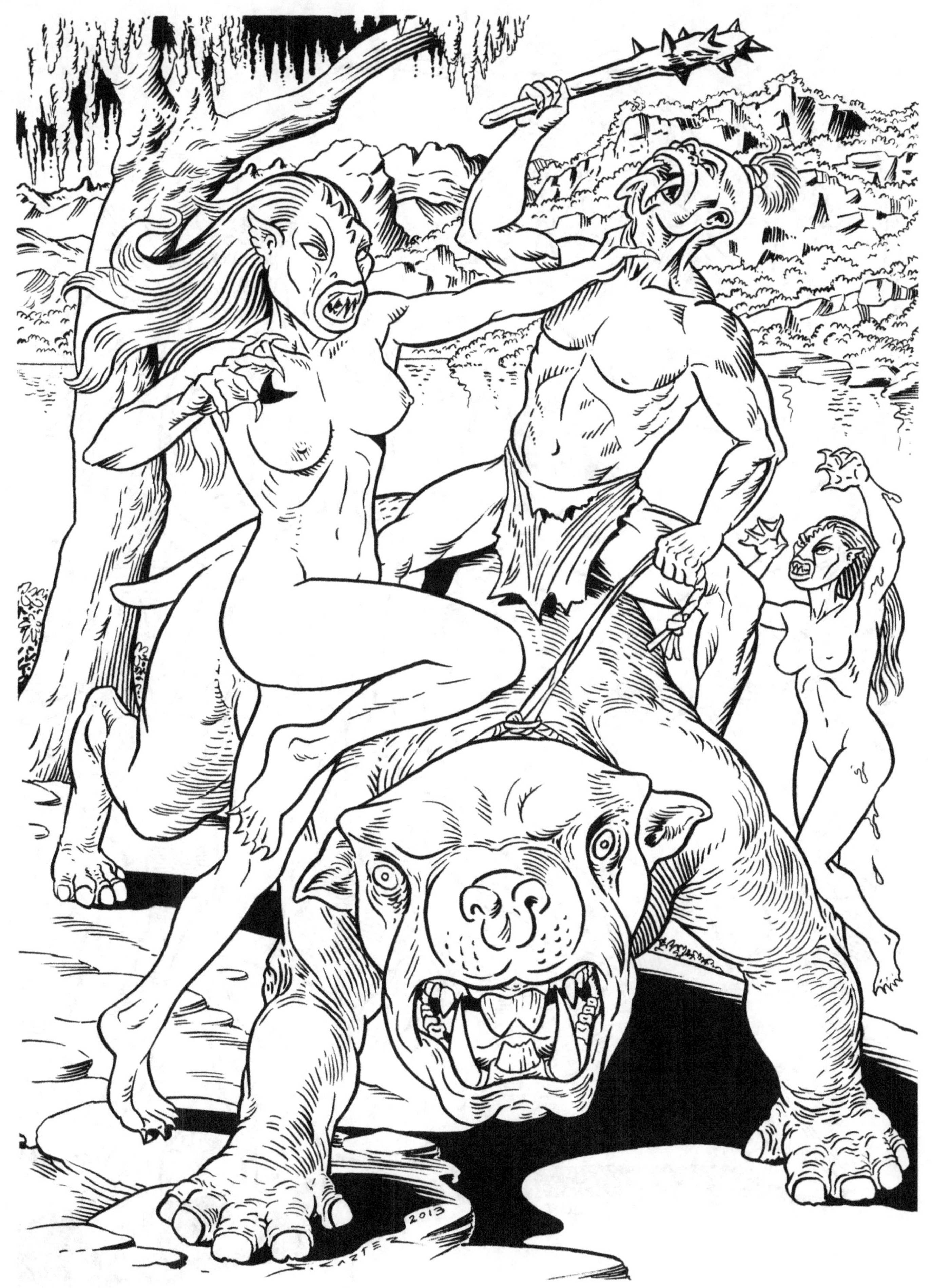

Riverside Ambush

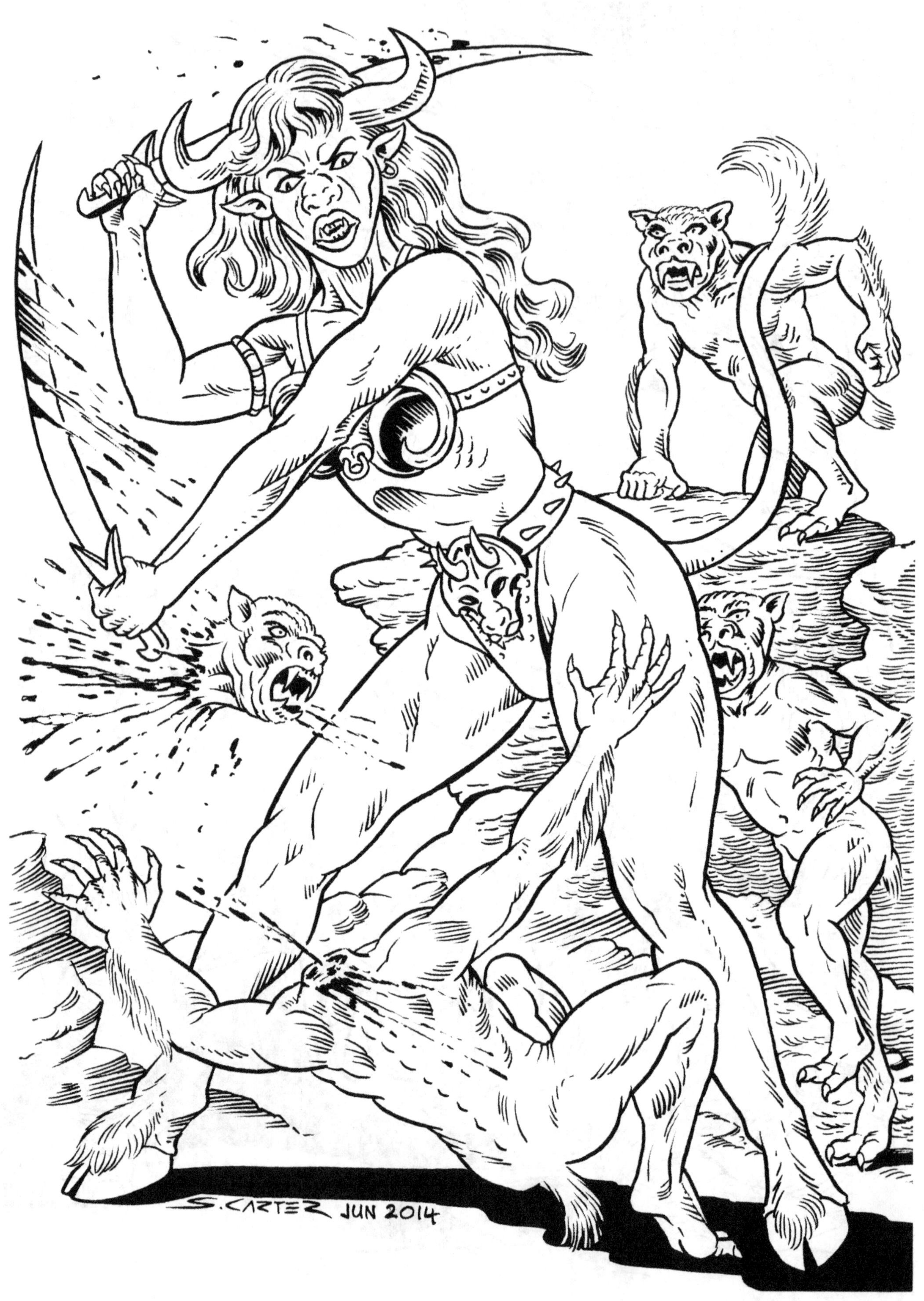

Giant Gynotaur War Goddess Slaughters the Sabre-Tooth Clan

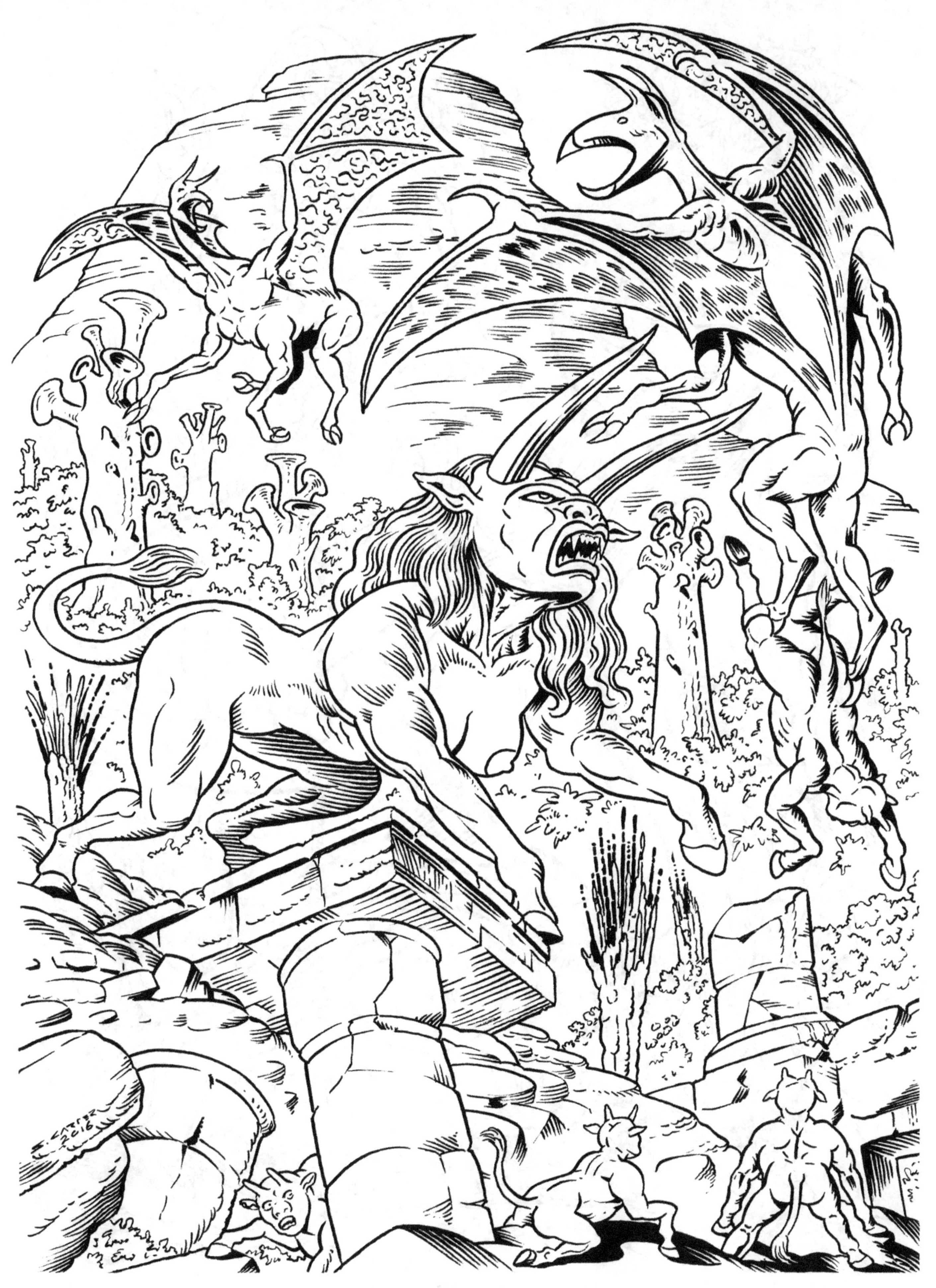

Hurgulon Defending her Cubs

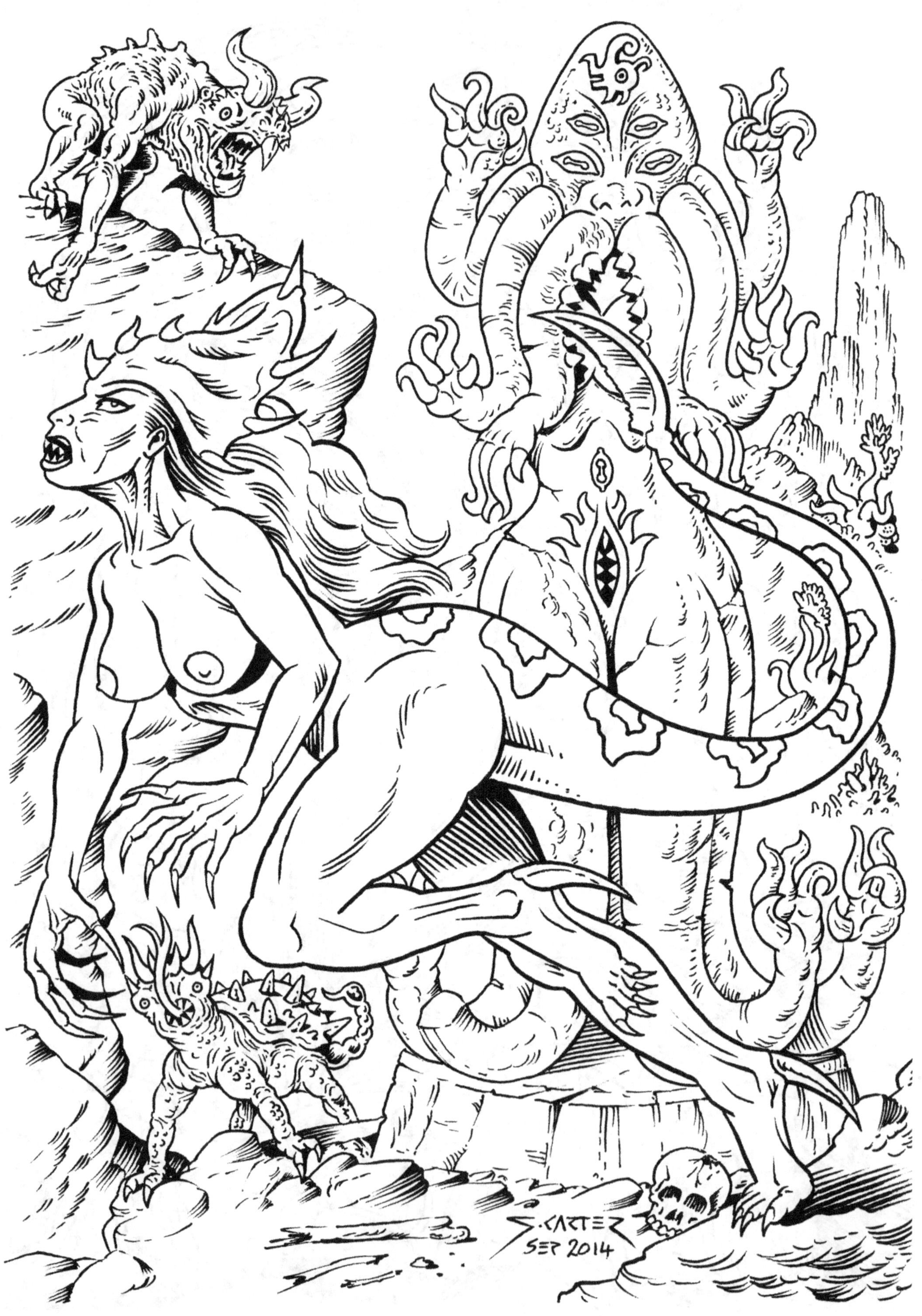

**A Frill-Headed Blood Hooker
sprints in front of the statue of The Malevolent Goddess 'Maguukah'**

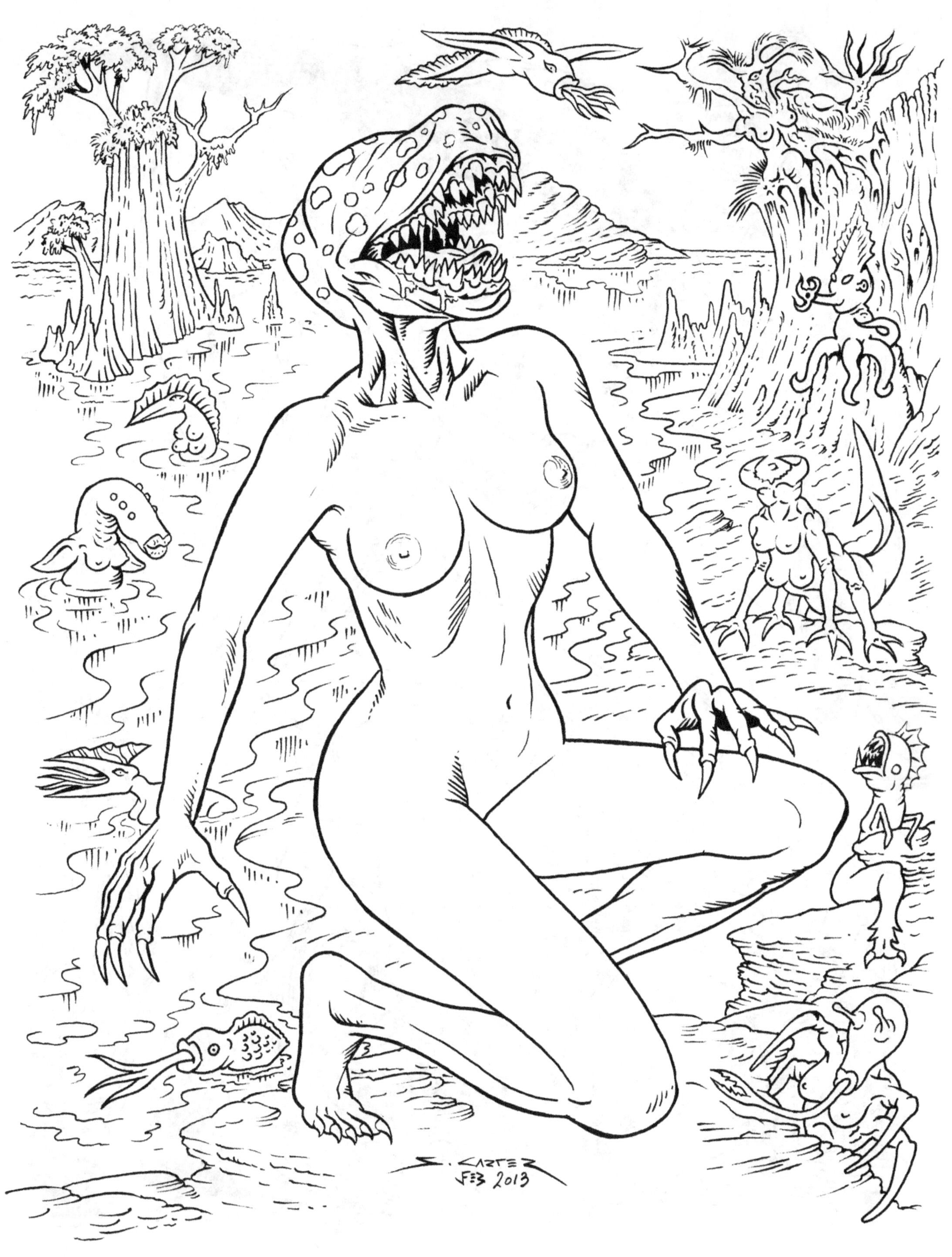

Dentata Spawnorg
and Other Indefinable Gynorgs

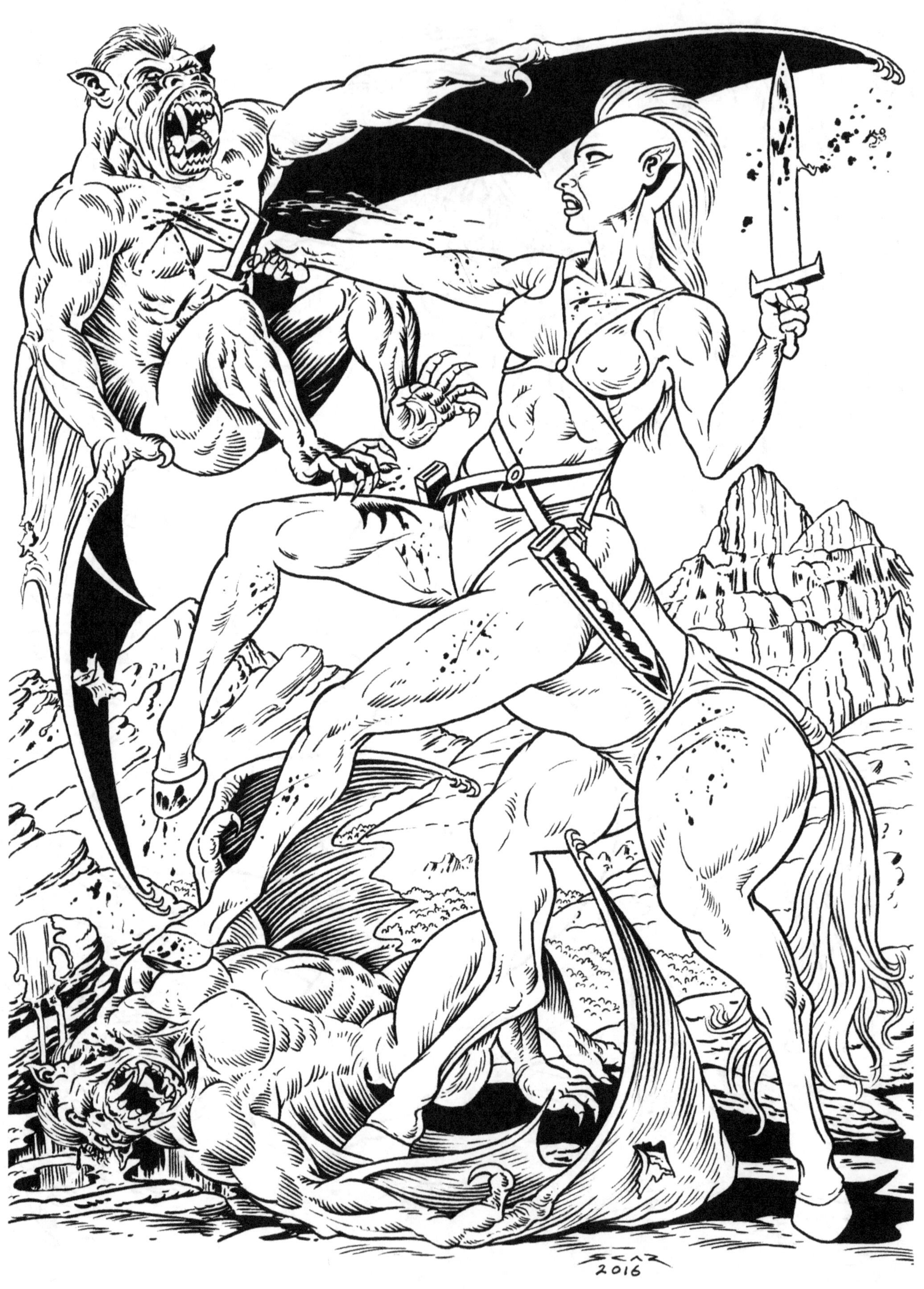

Amazonian Centrix Fights to Defend her Virtue

DARE YOU FACE THE...
WRATH OF M'BUBU!
DEMON-DEVIL OF DEEPEST, DARKEST MONGO-GONGO LAND!

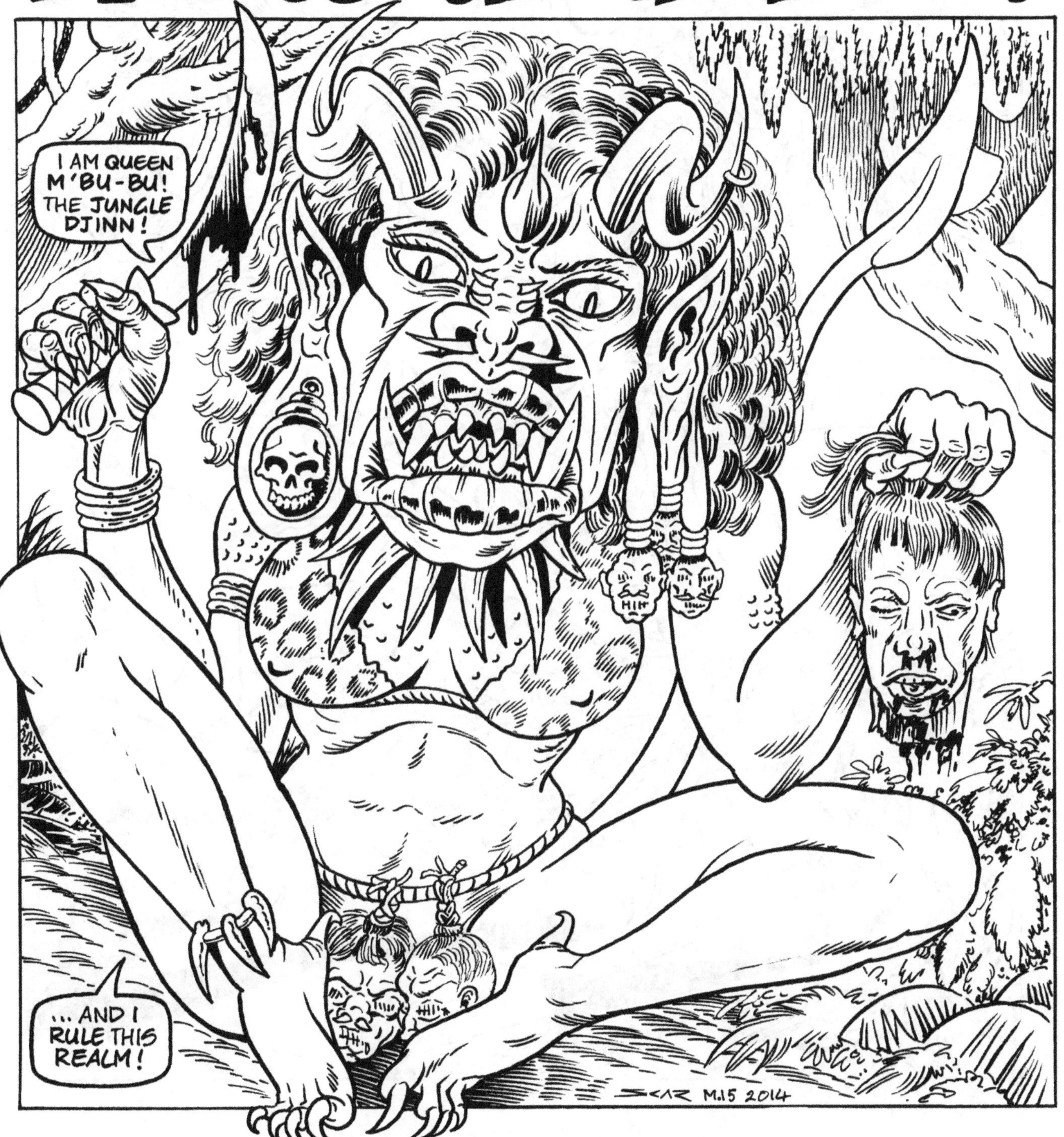

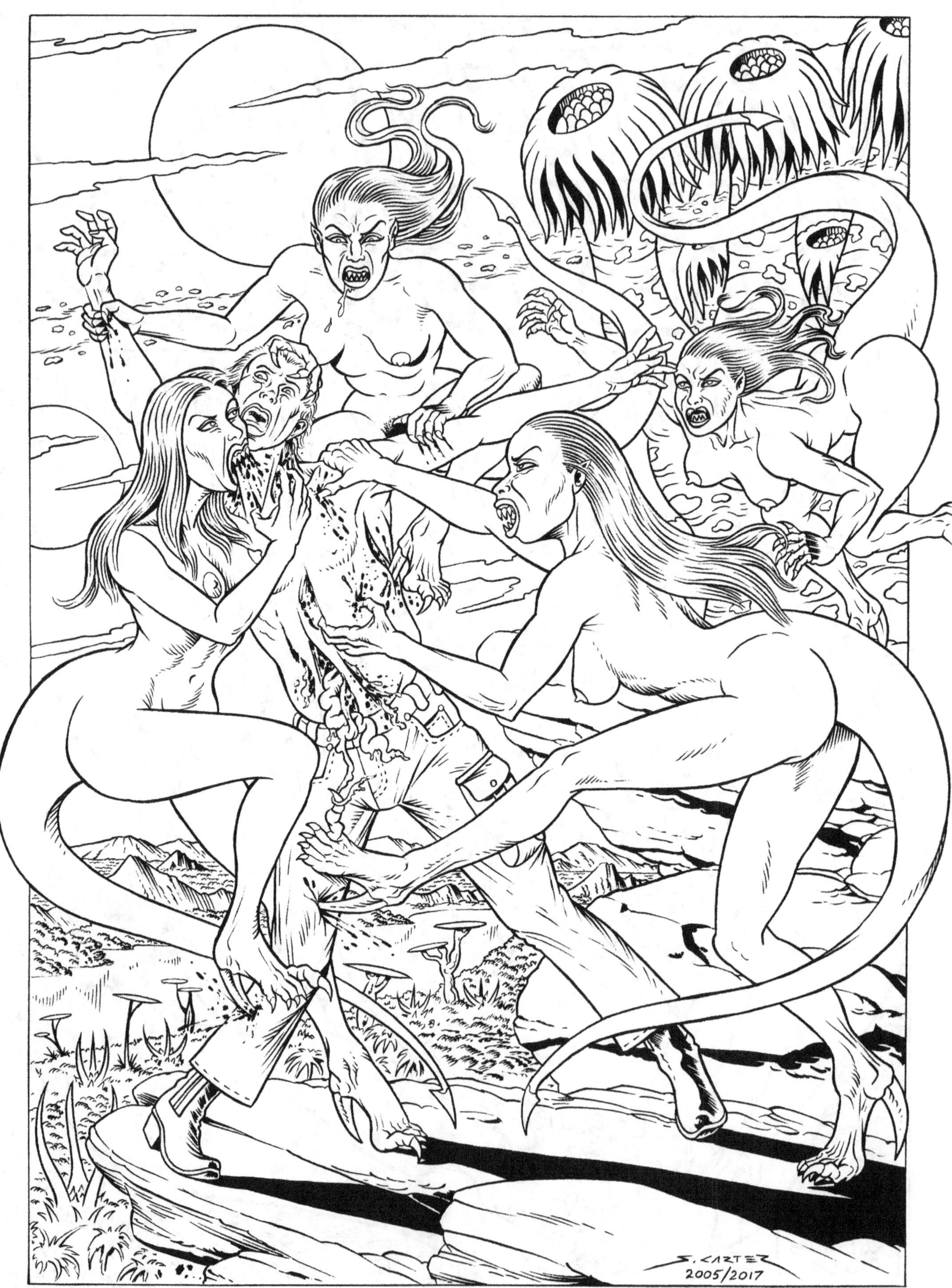

Fem Raptor Fury

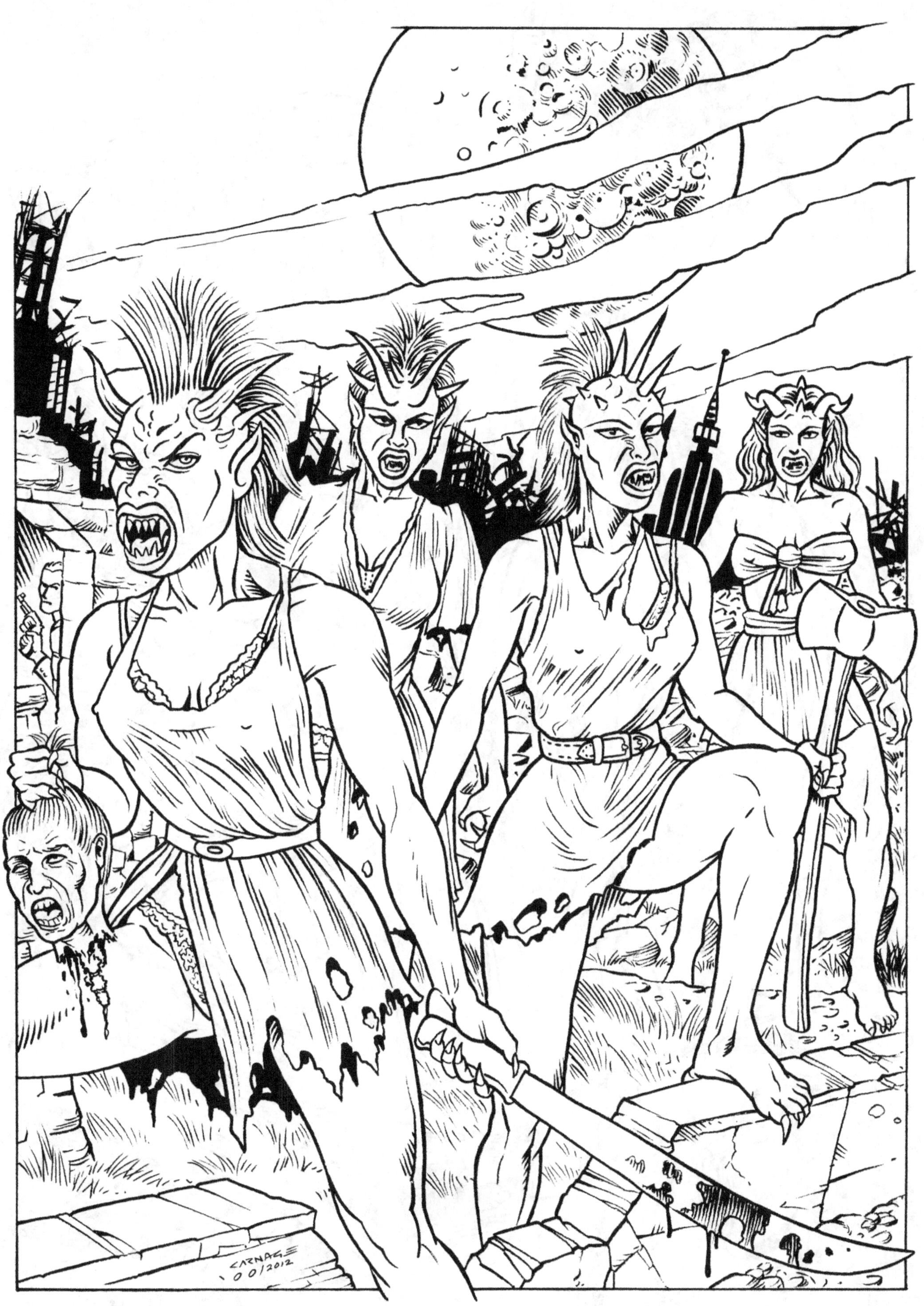

Rampage of the Troll Dolls

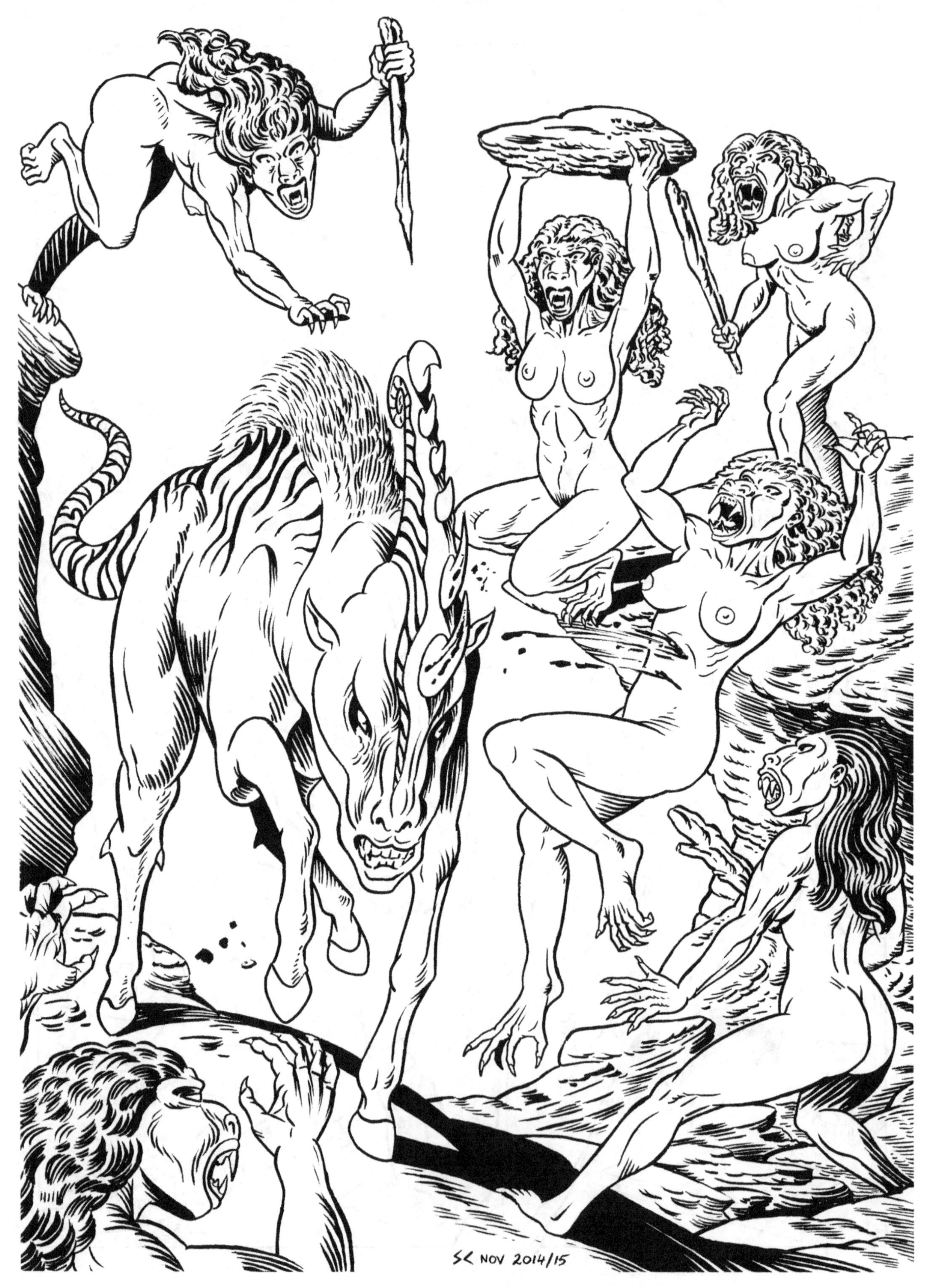

Hunting Trollops Must Eat

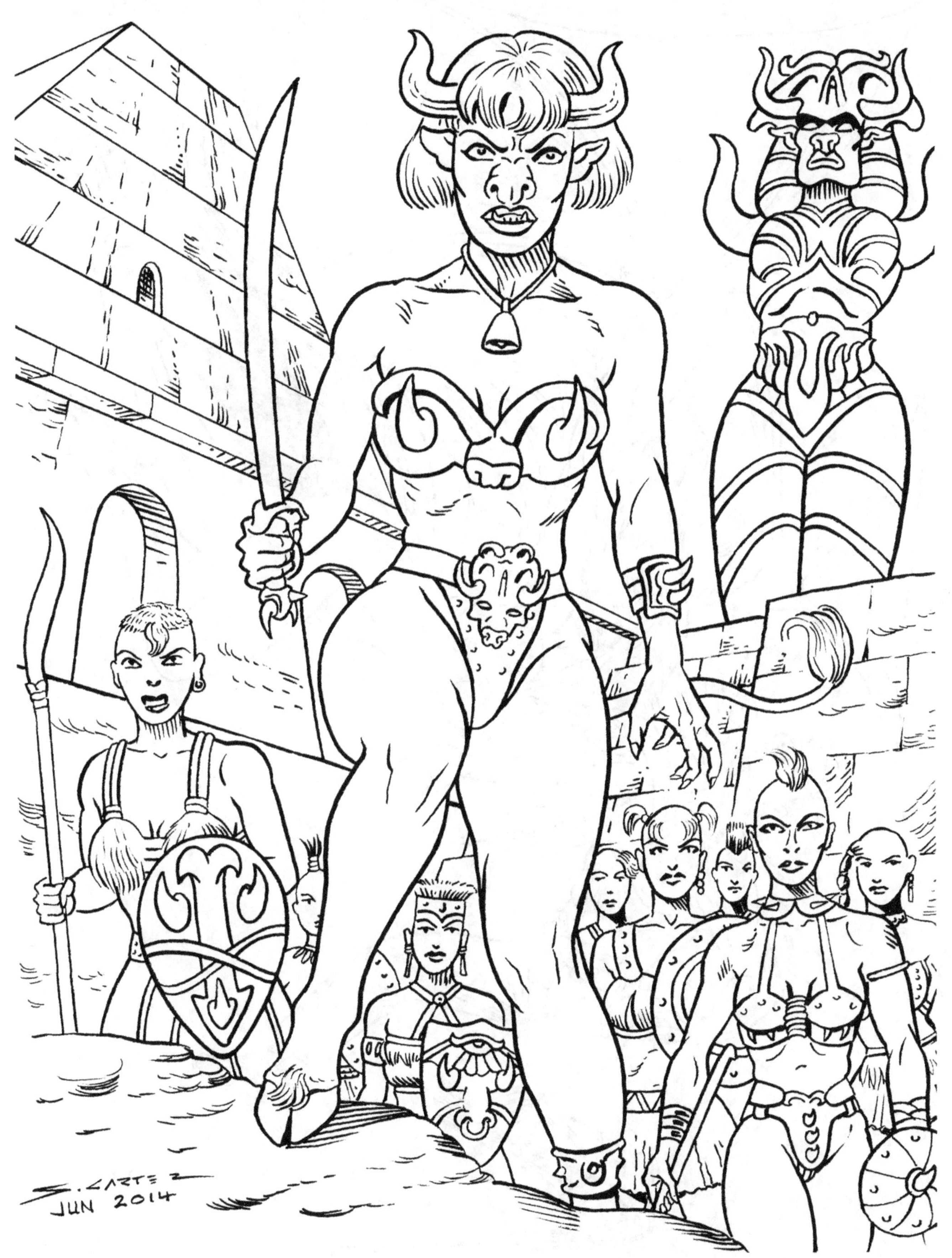

The Militant Devotees of Tauria Assemble a War Party

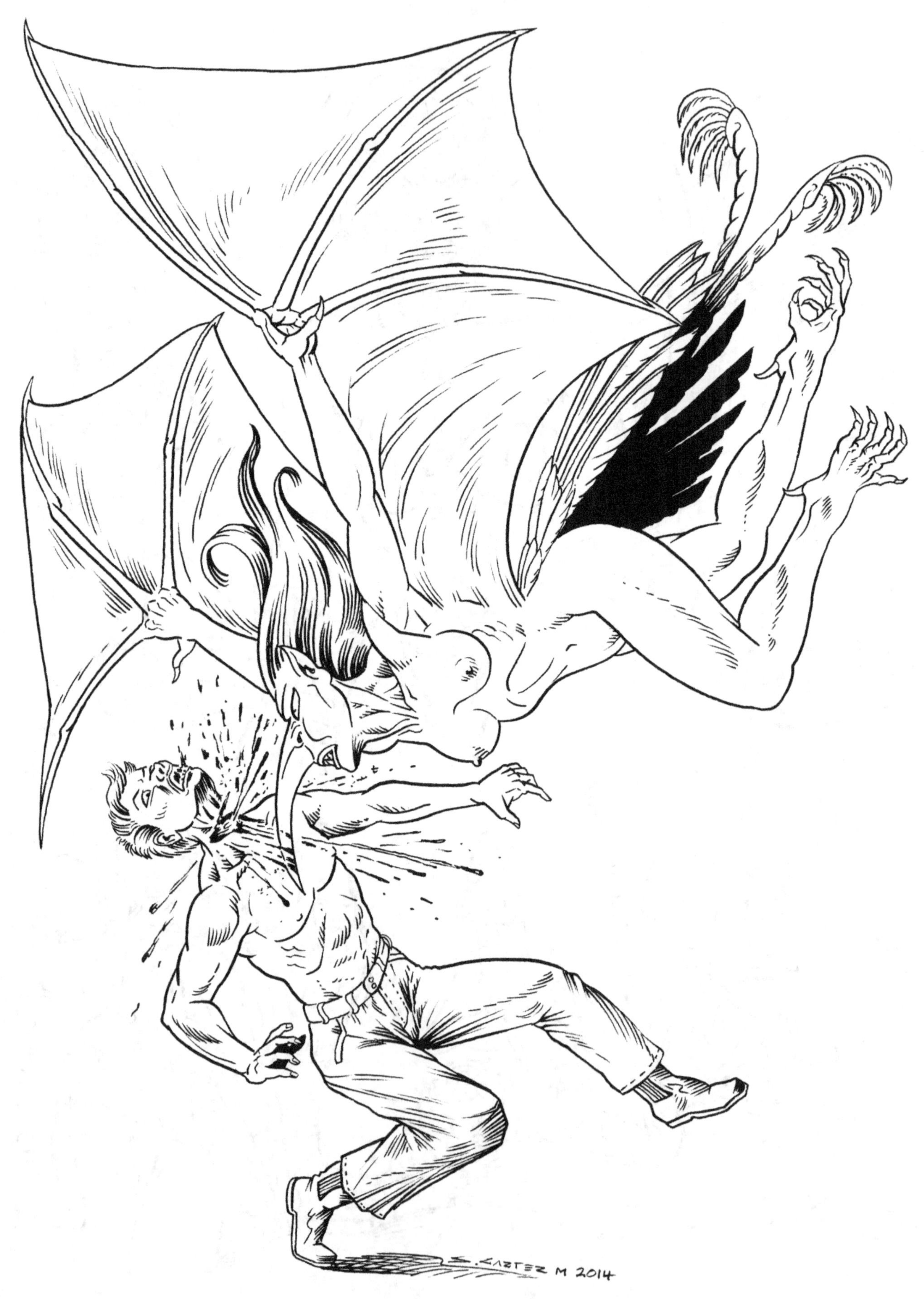

Scythe-Nosed Harpyopteryx Strikes

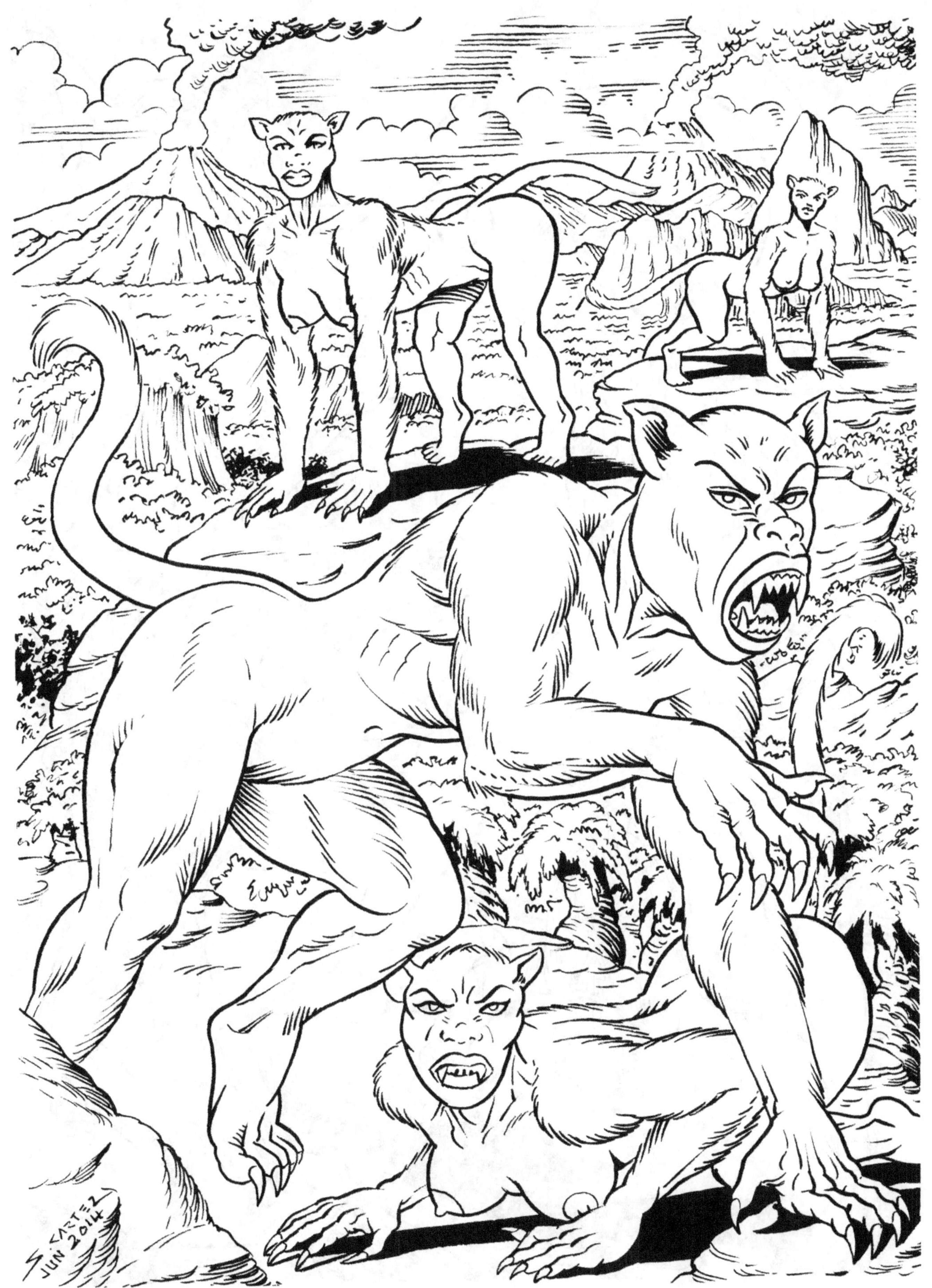

Pride of Sphinxes

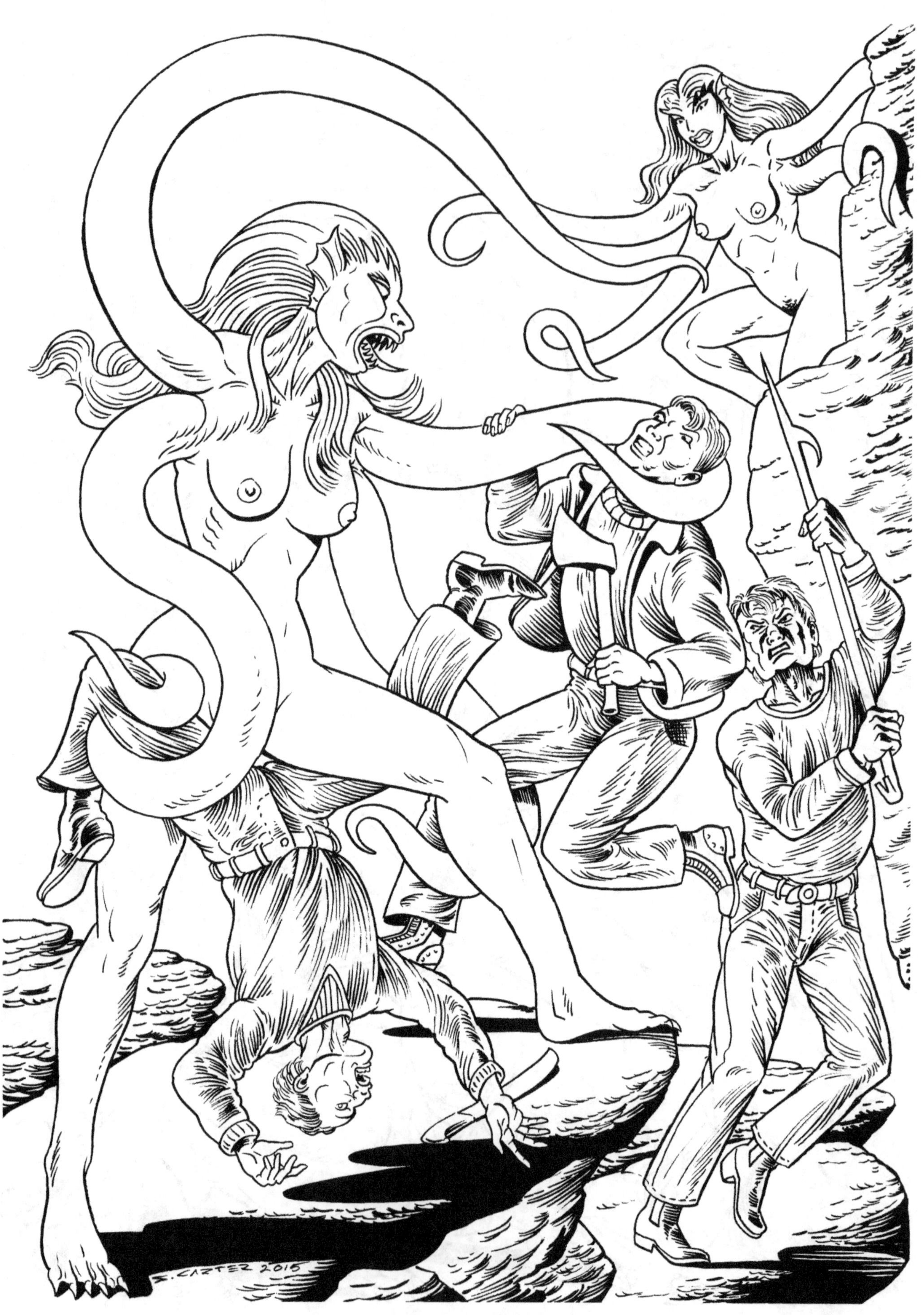

Sirens from Saturn

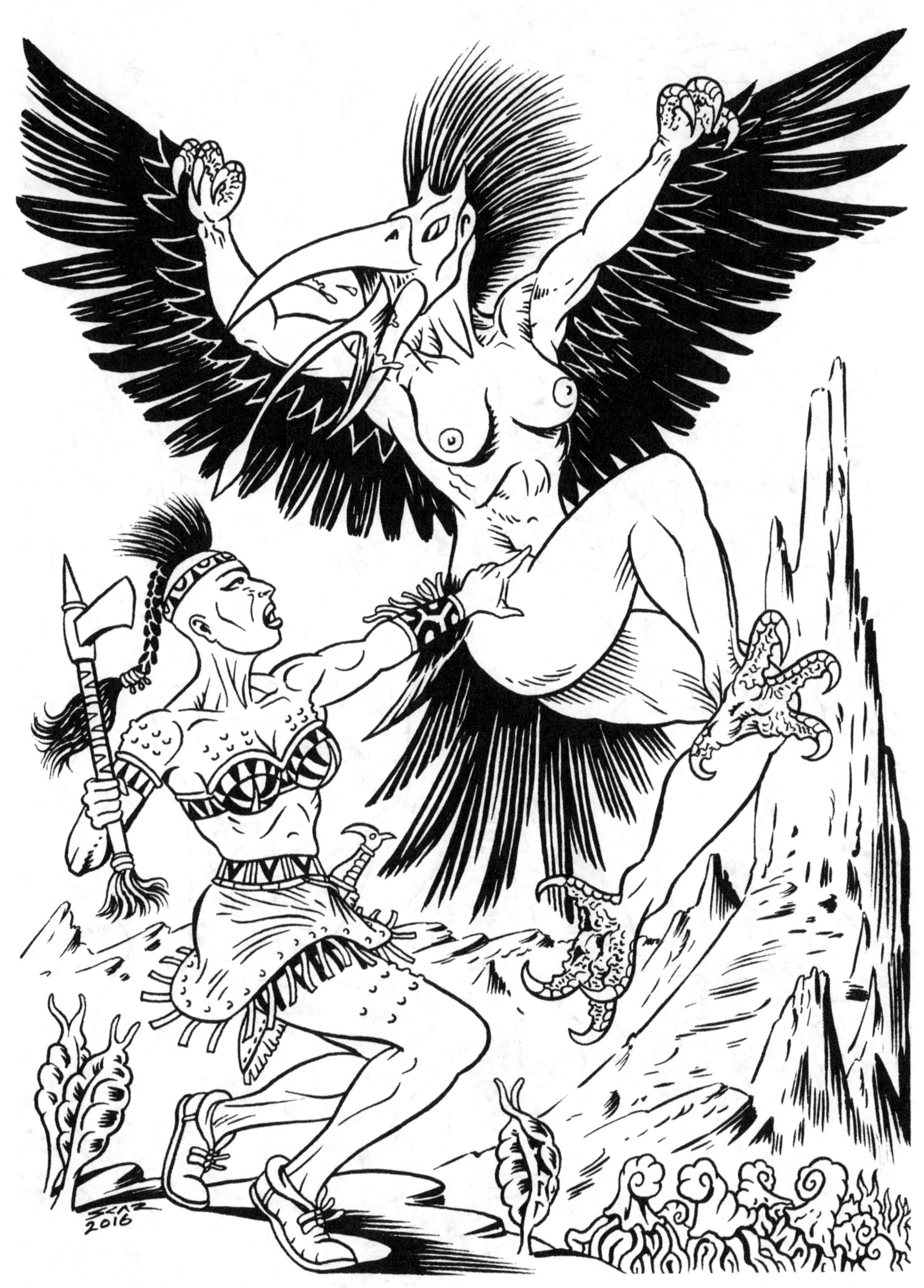

Menace of the She-Crow

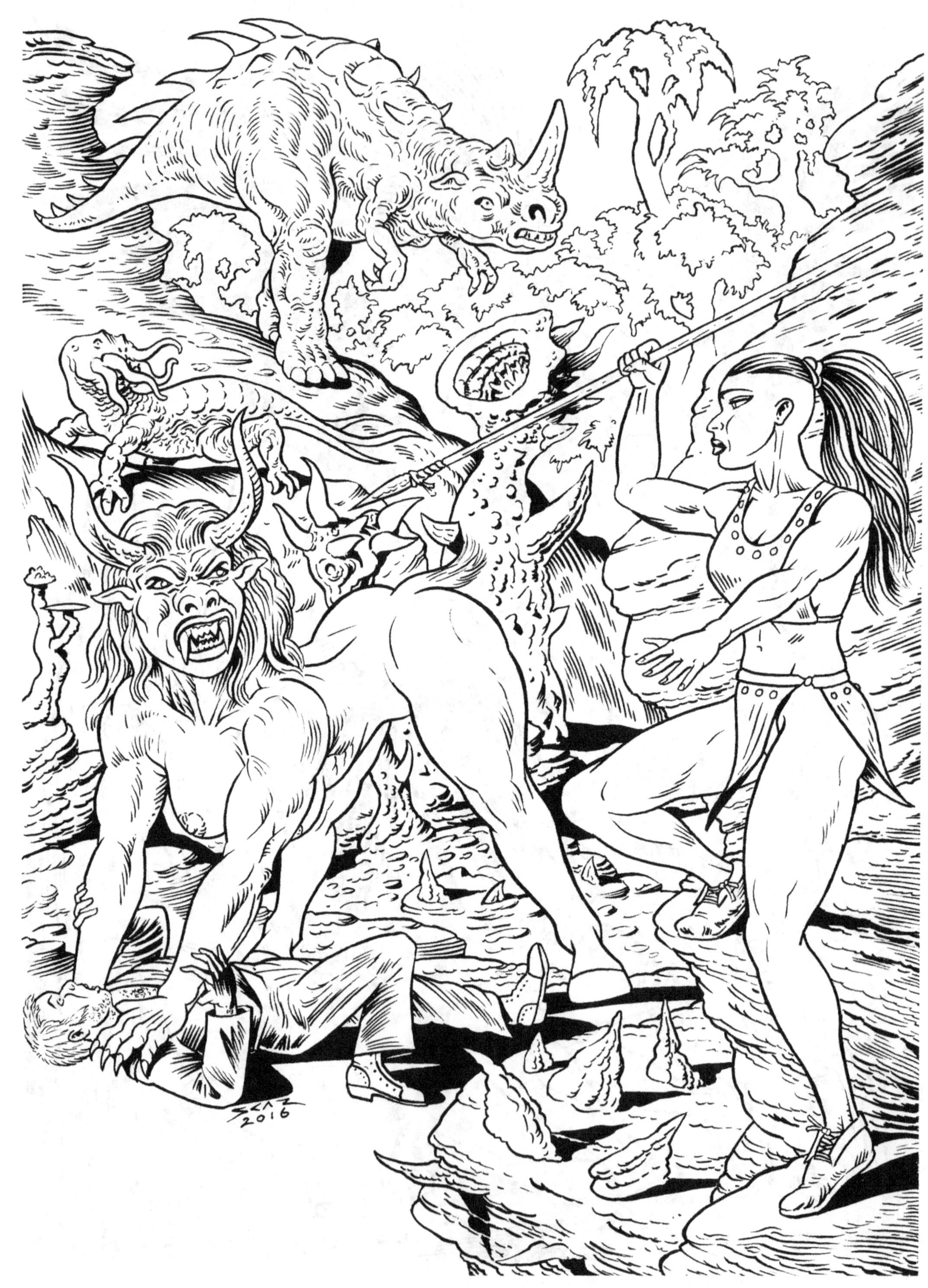

Deadly She Devil

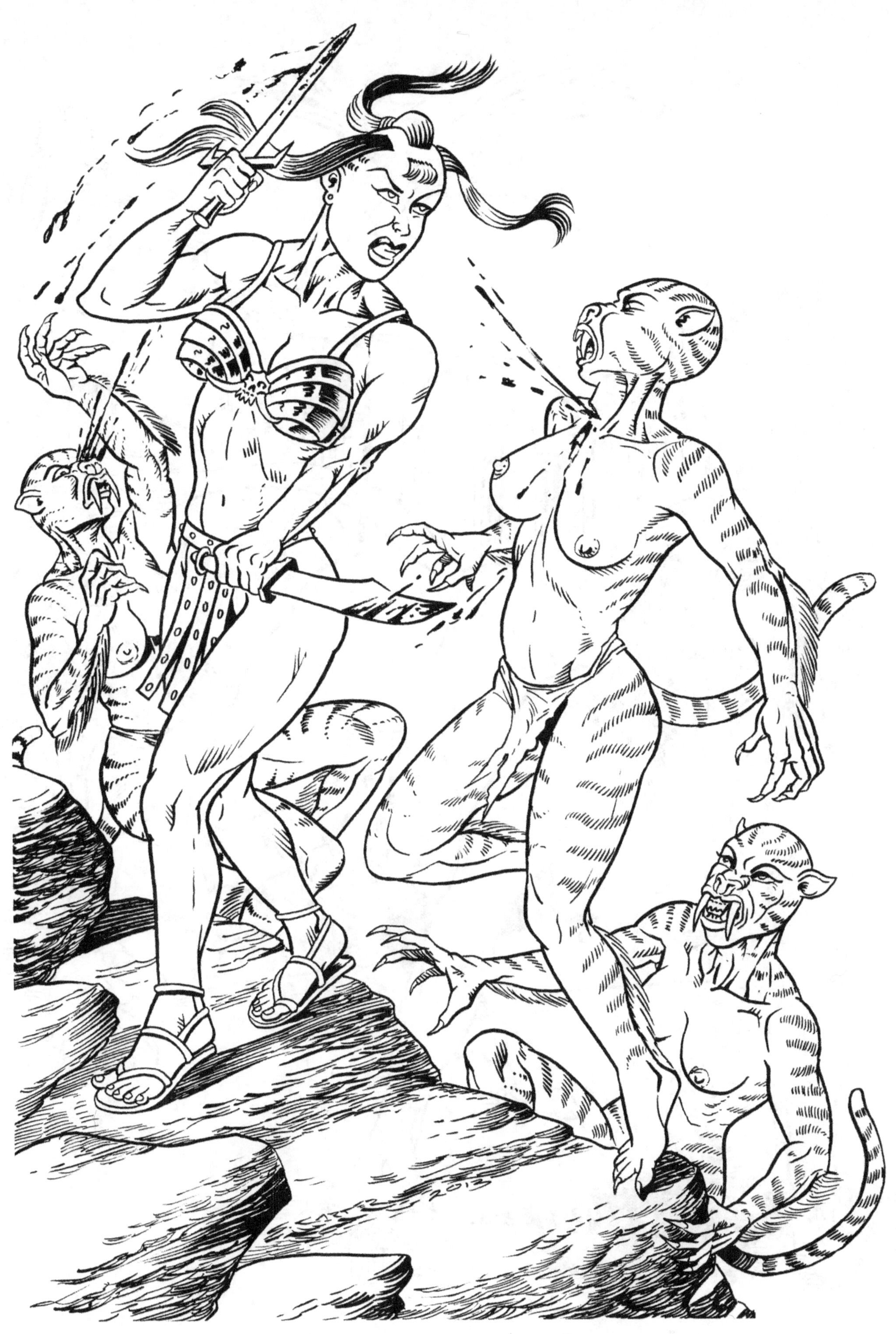

Sabre Tooth Tigress Cult

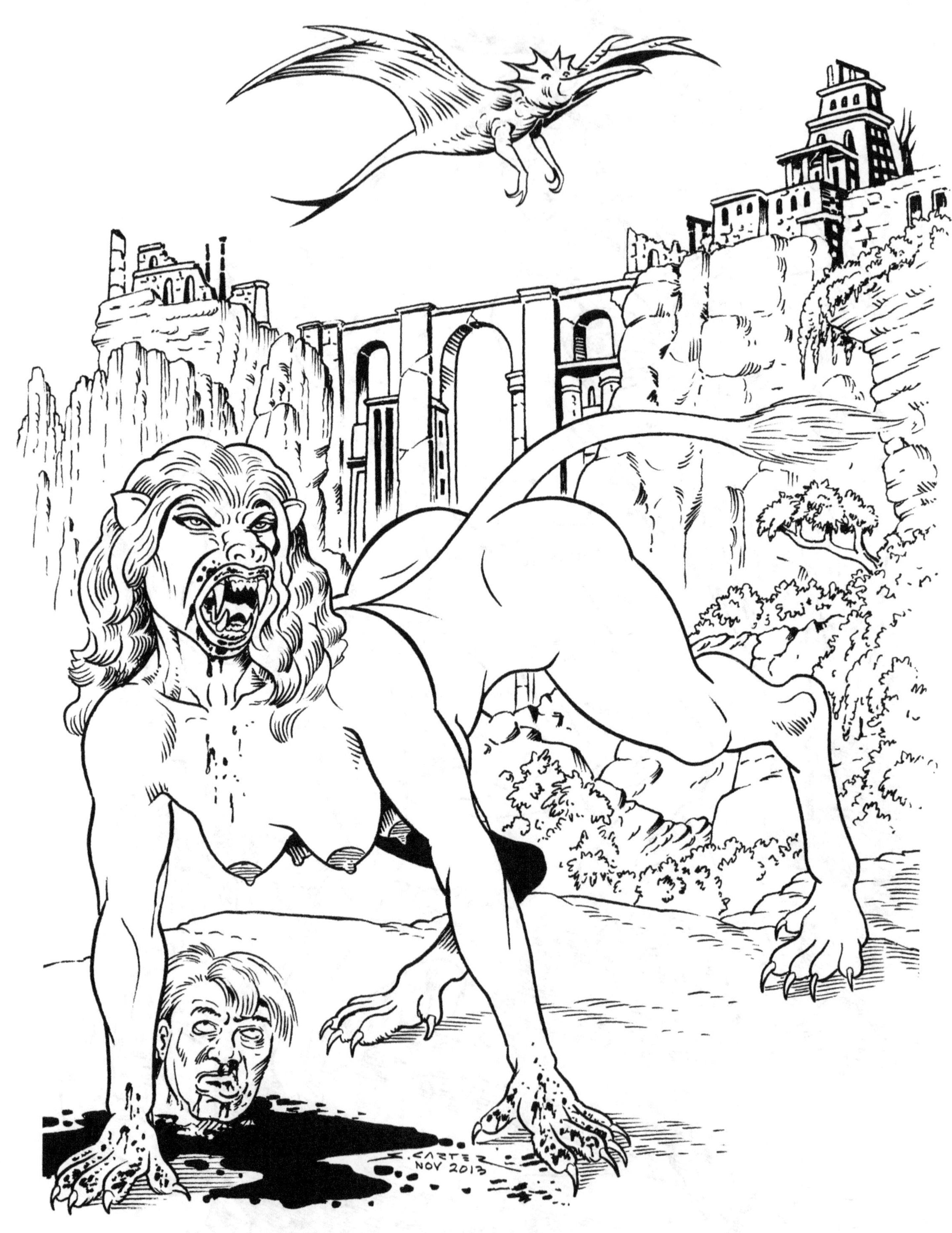

Six-Breasted Nemesean Sphinx and Trophy

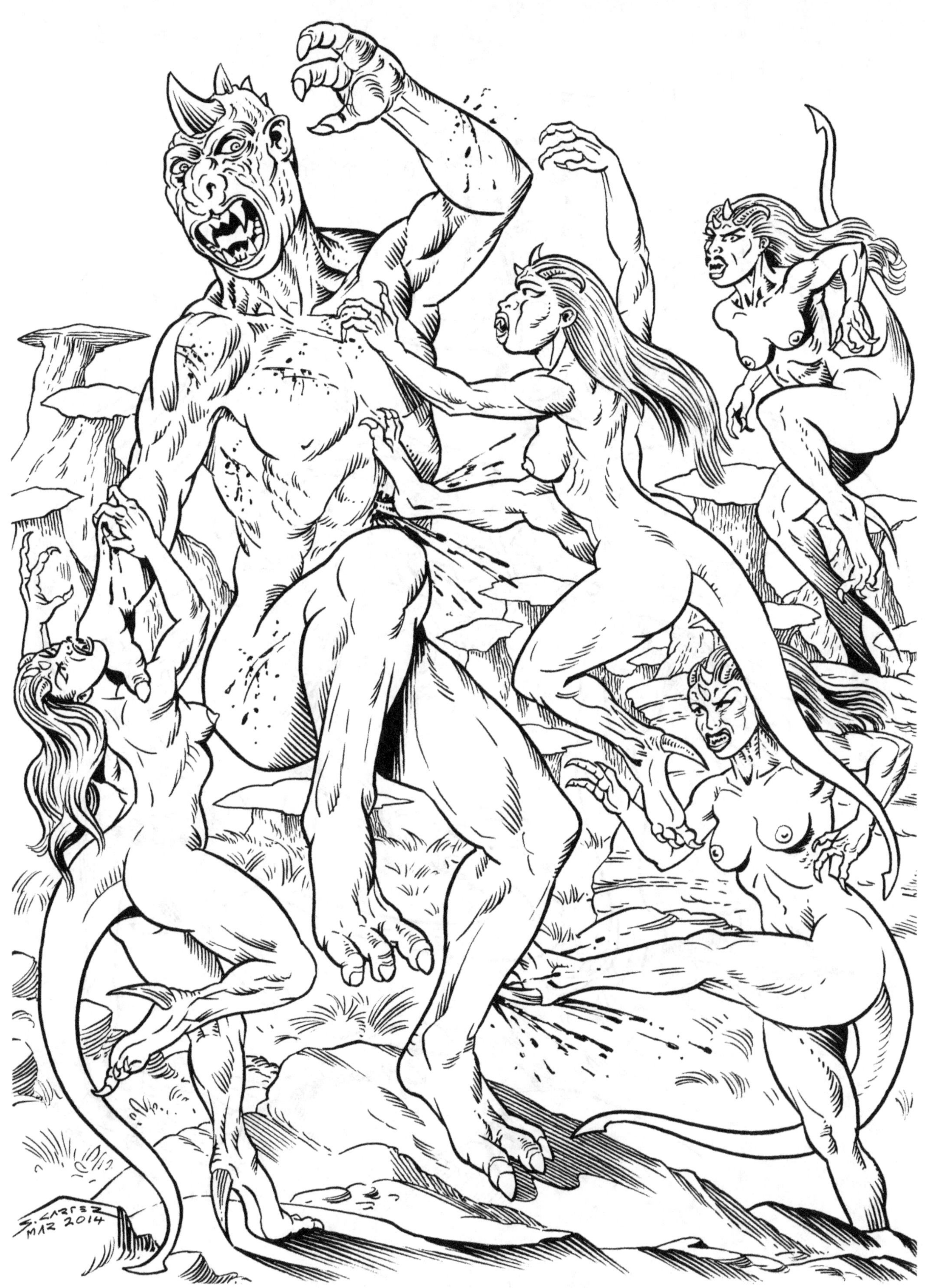

Fem Raptor Frenzy

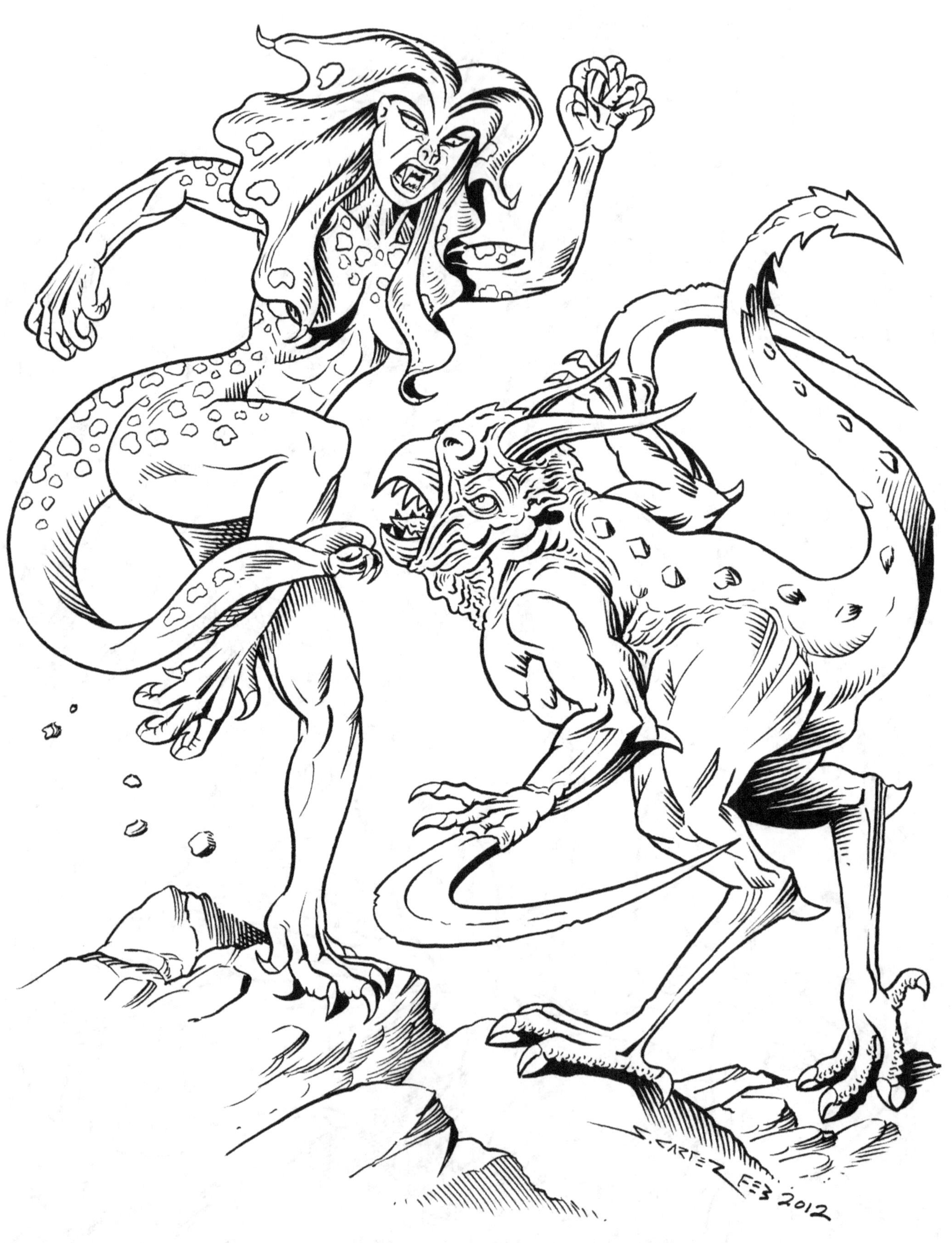

Basilisk versus Sleth

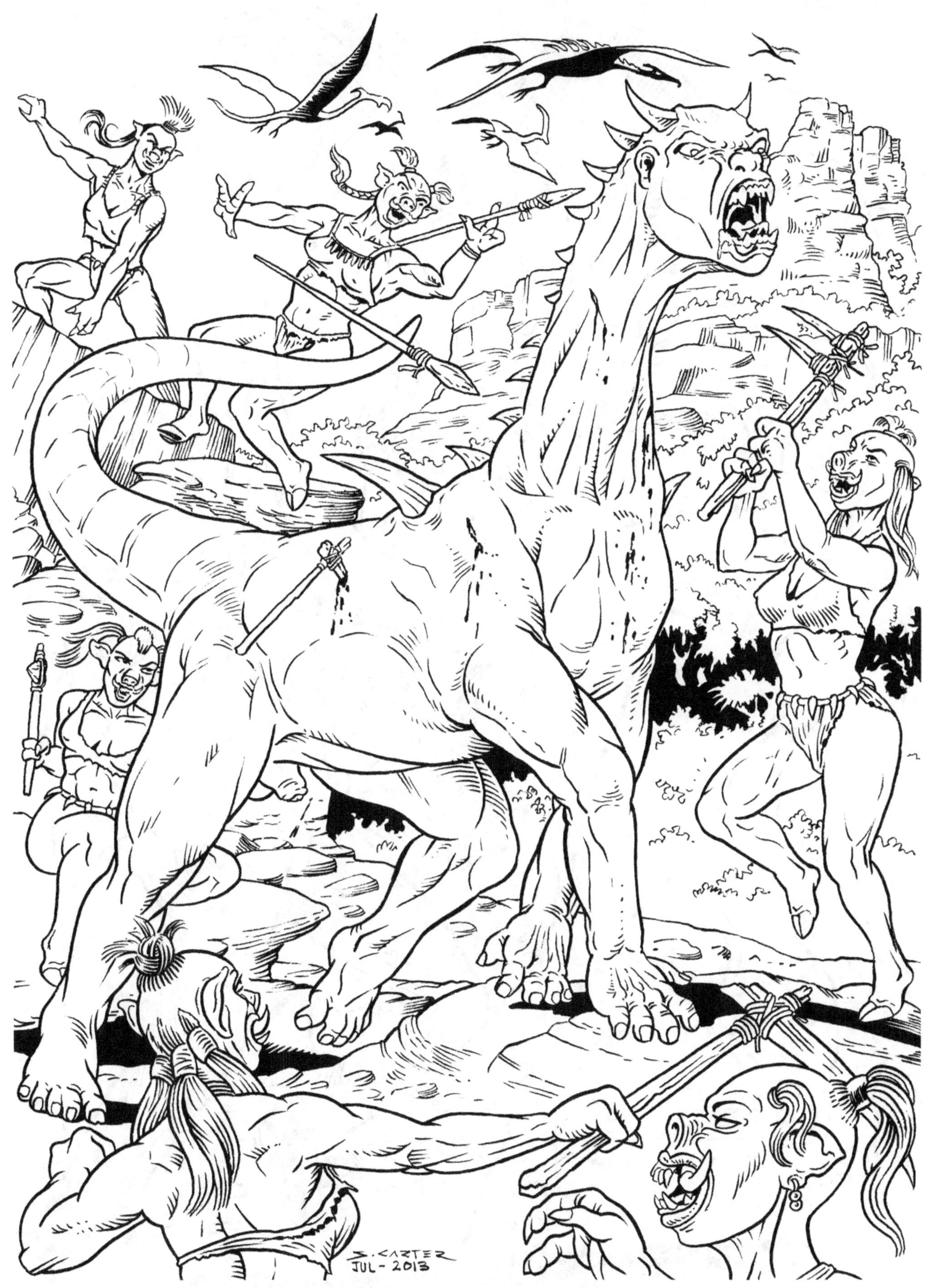

Tribal Hunters

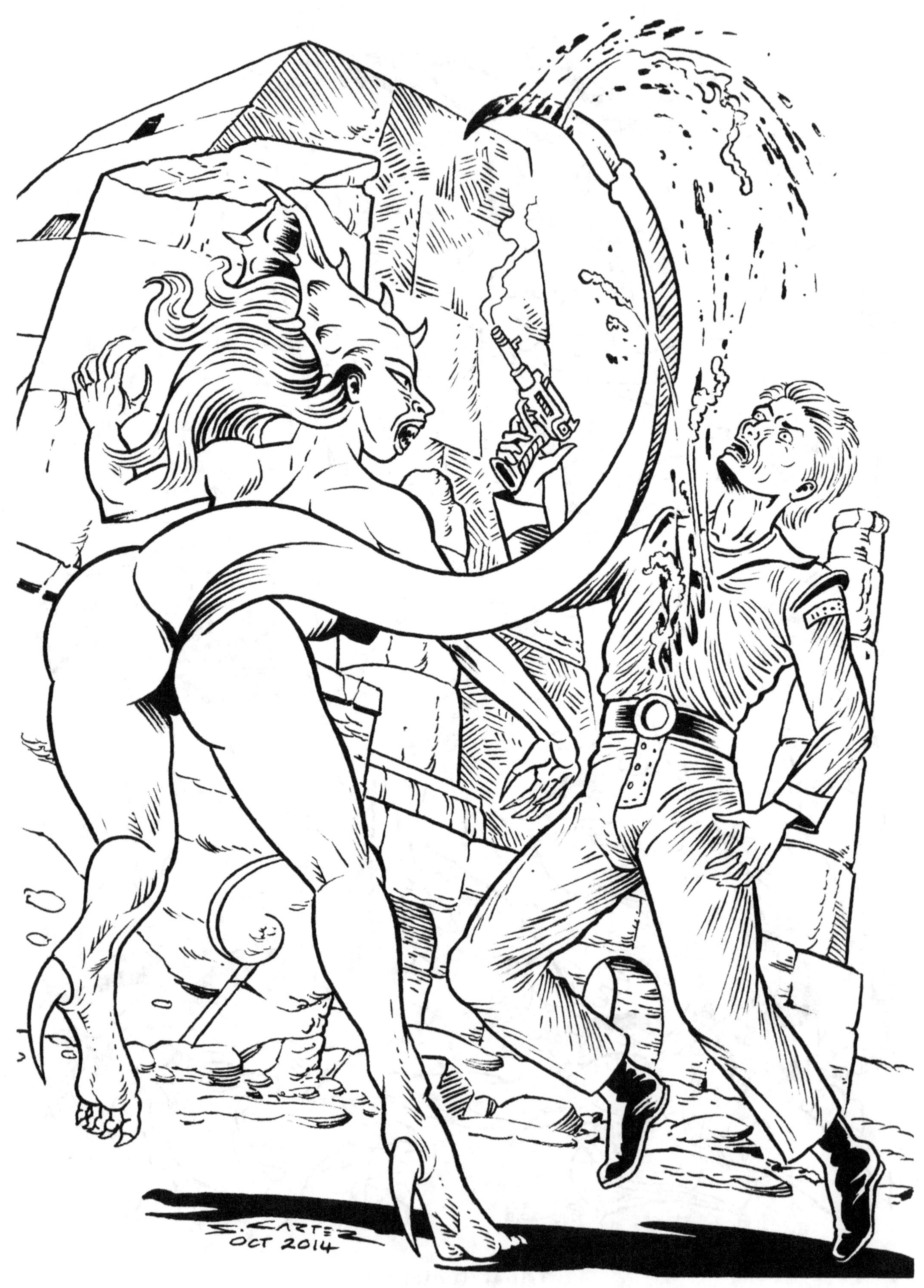

Evicerated by a Frill-Headed Blood Hooker

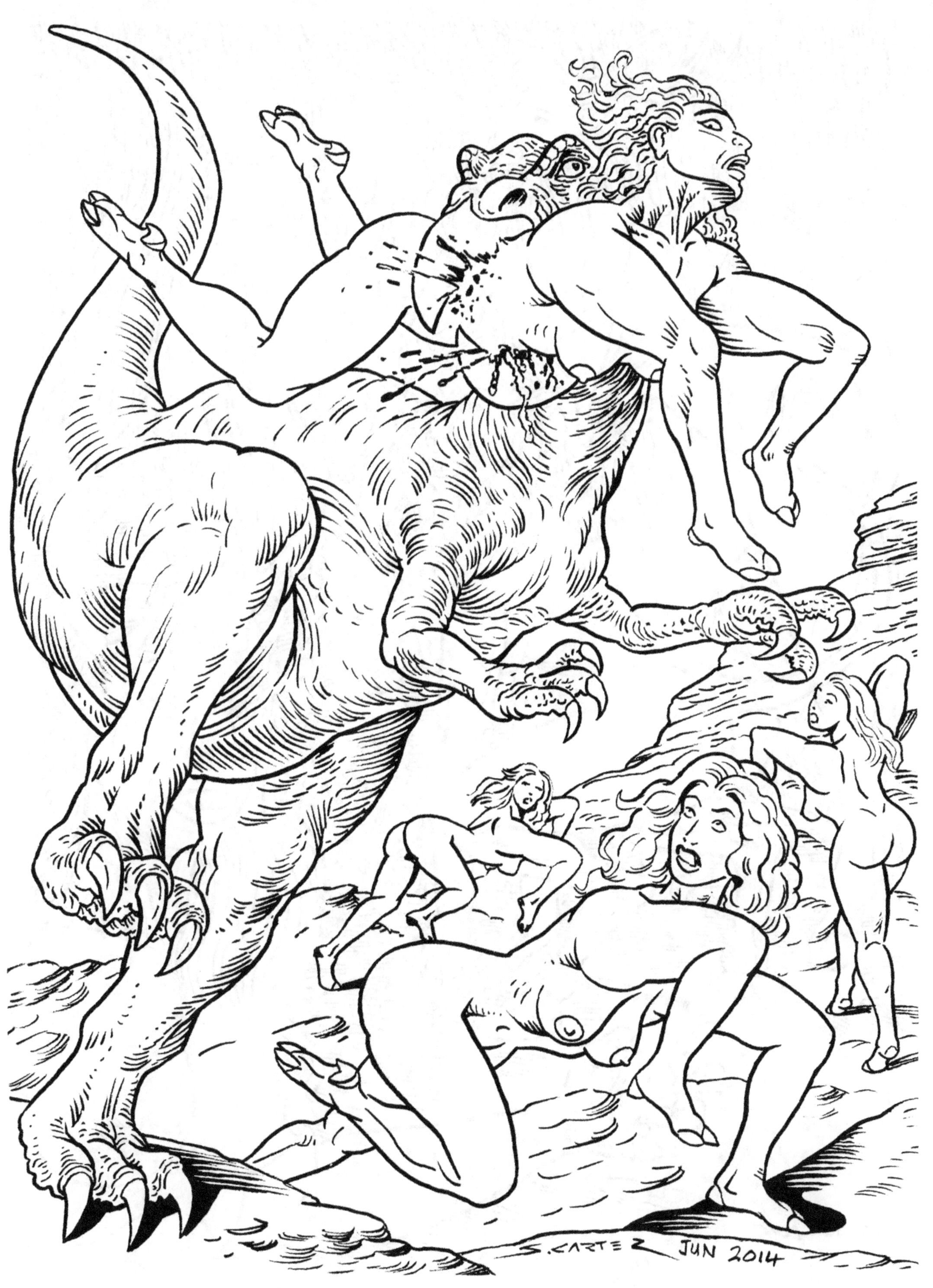

Femaquads Assailed by a Terror Beaked Saurian

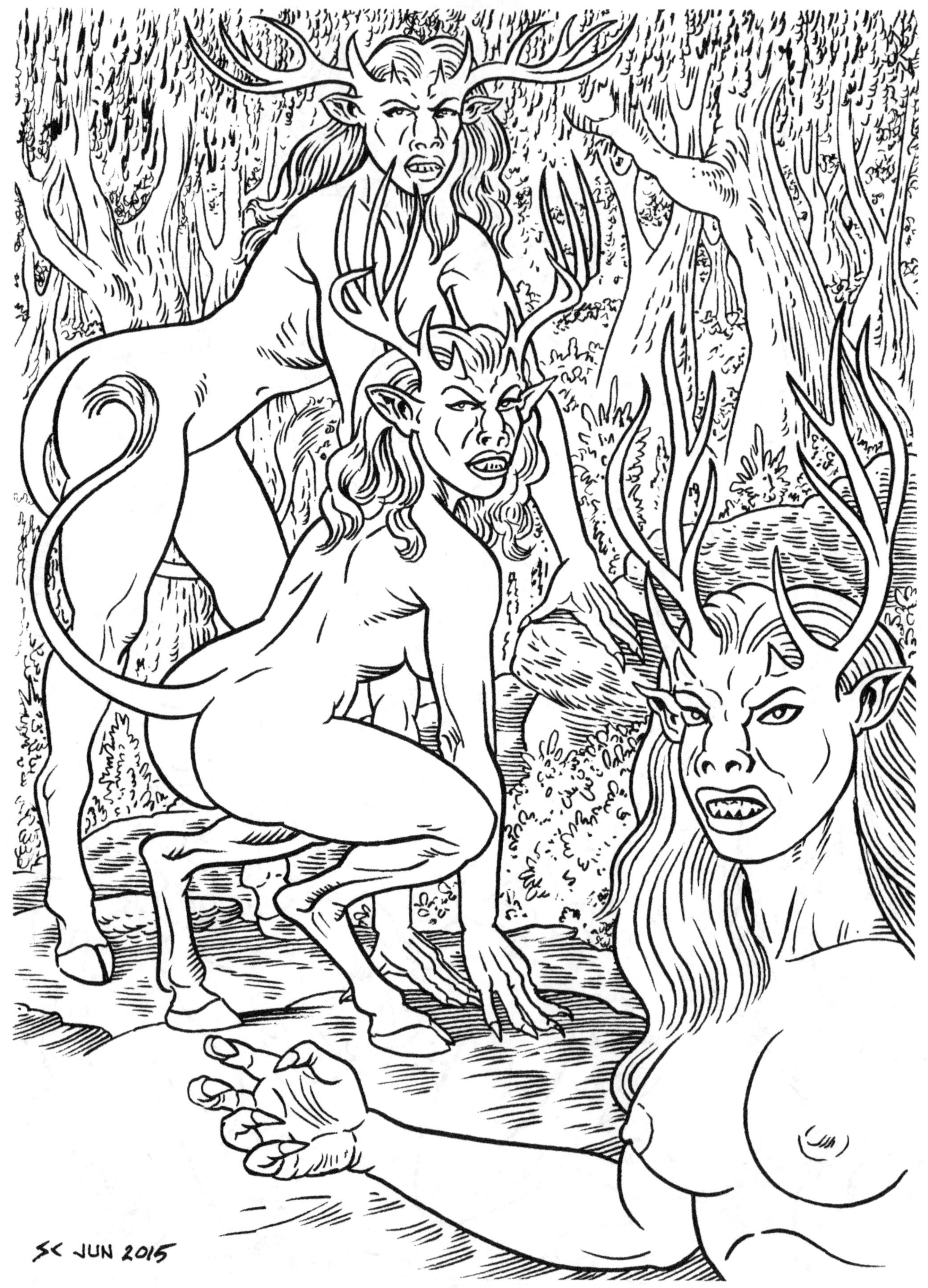

Wild Forest Trollops

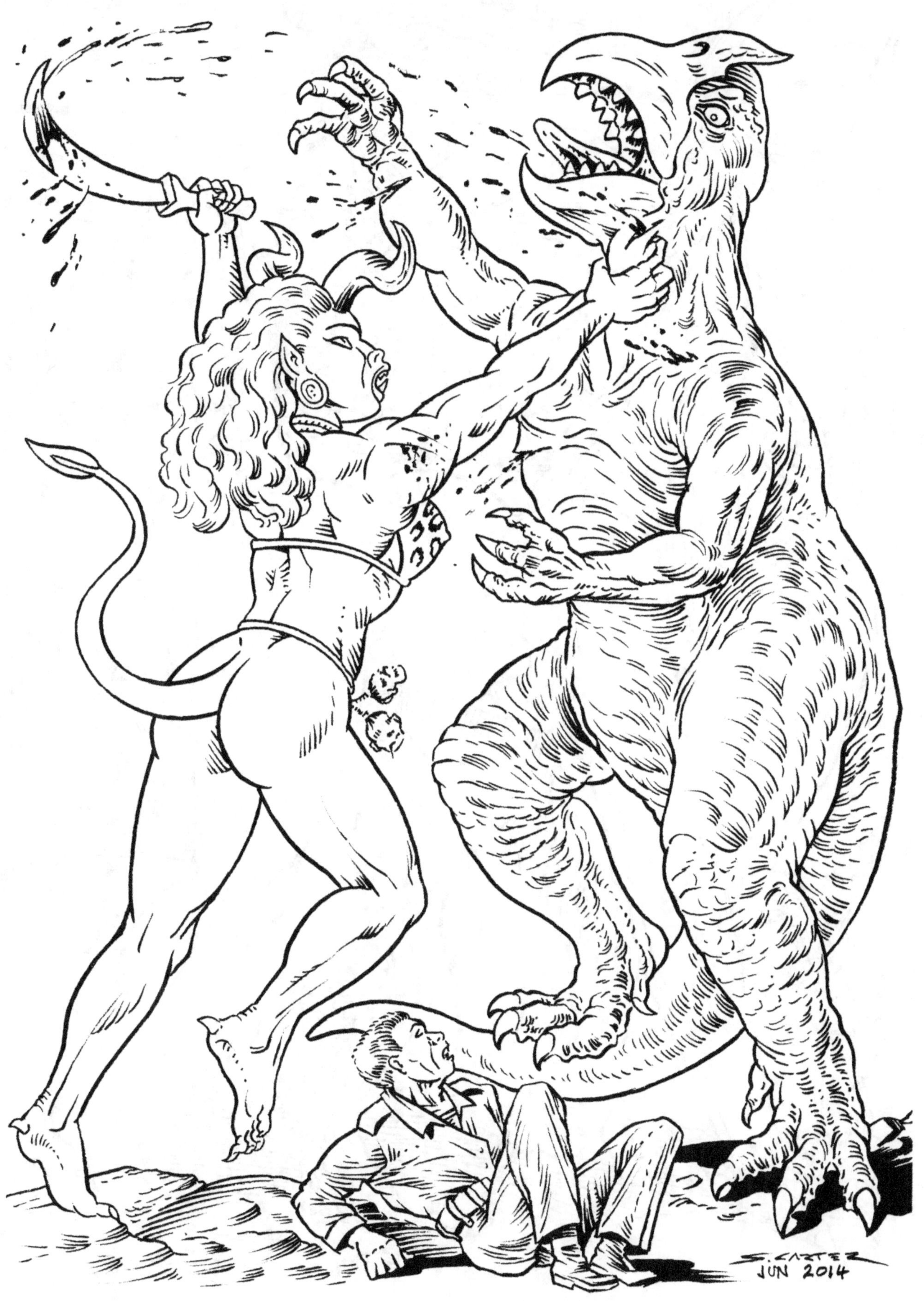

The Great M'Bu-Bu Battles Parrotosaur

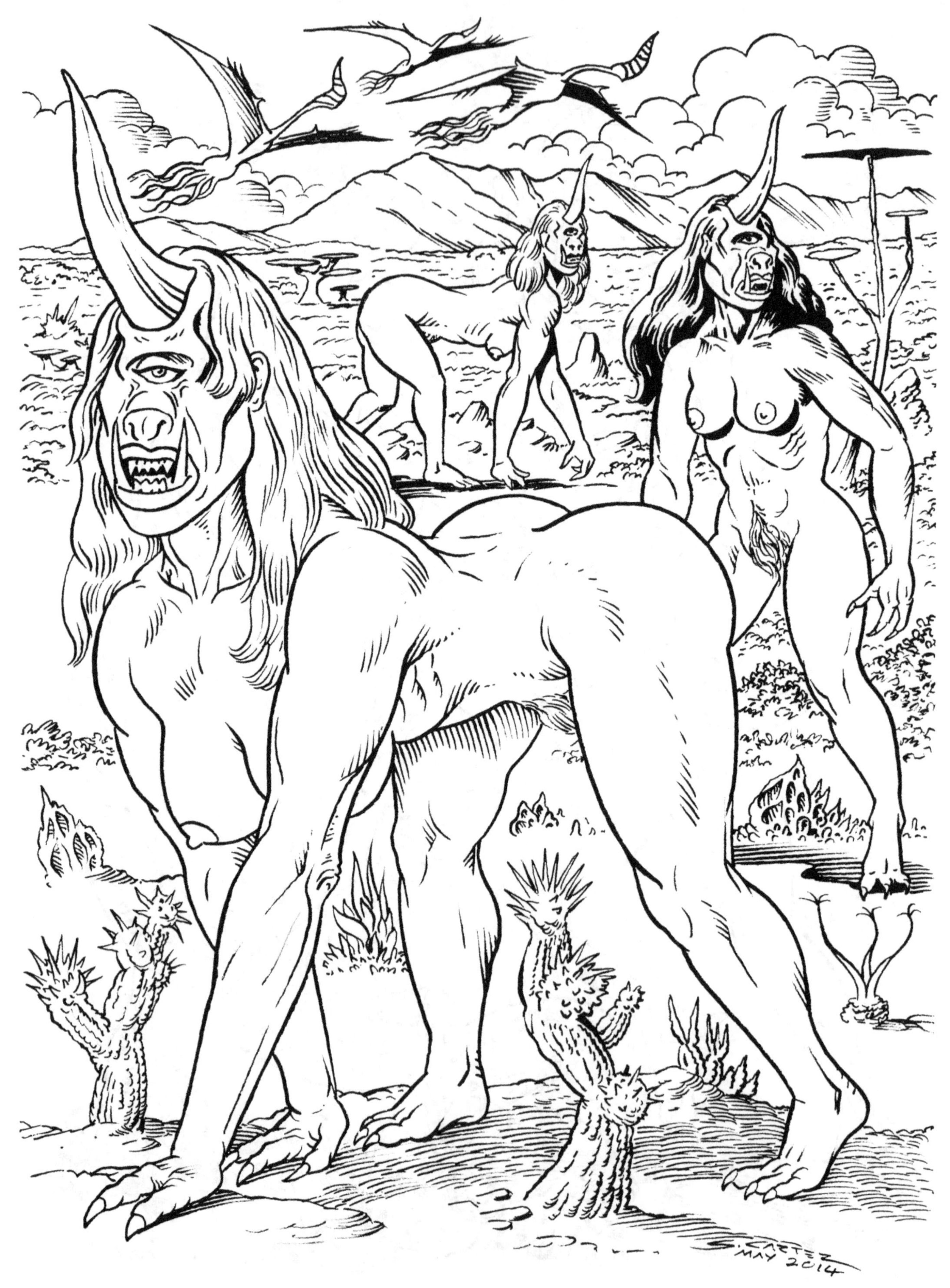

Giant Urps of the High Plains

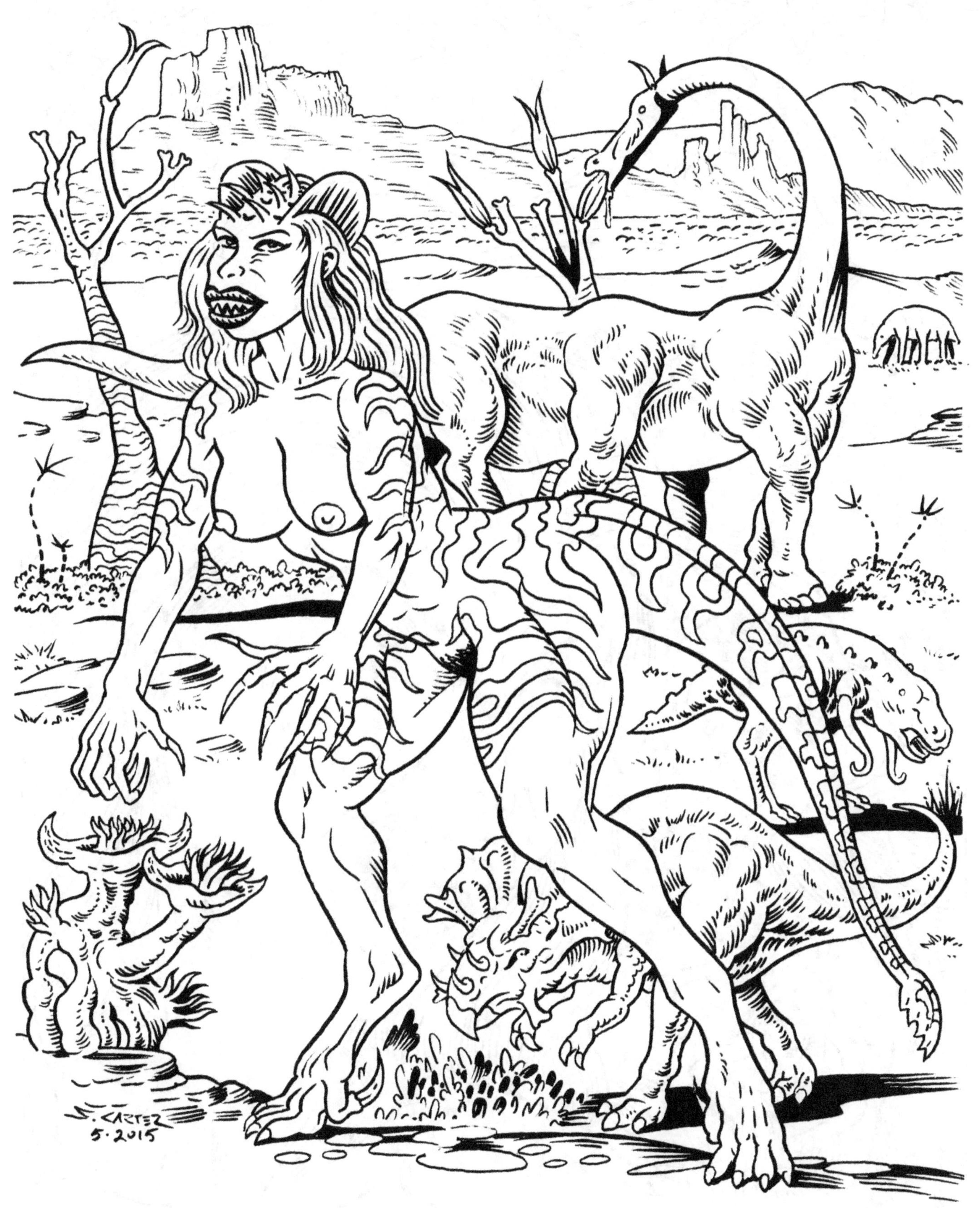

Hotlands Fem Raptor

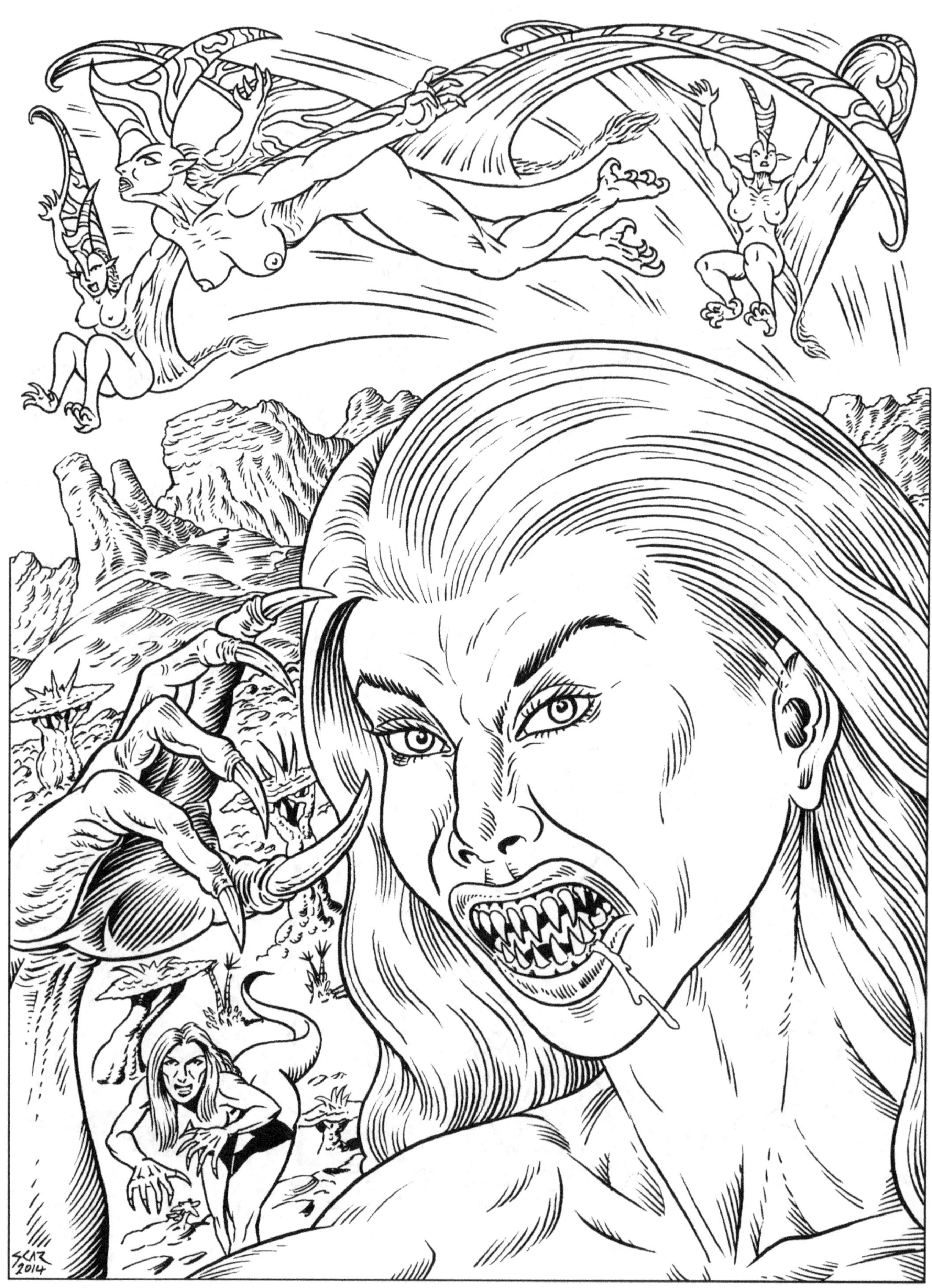

Designed to Kill

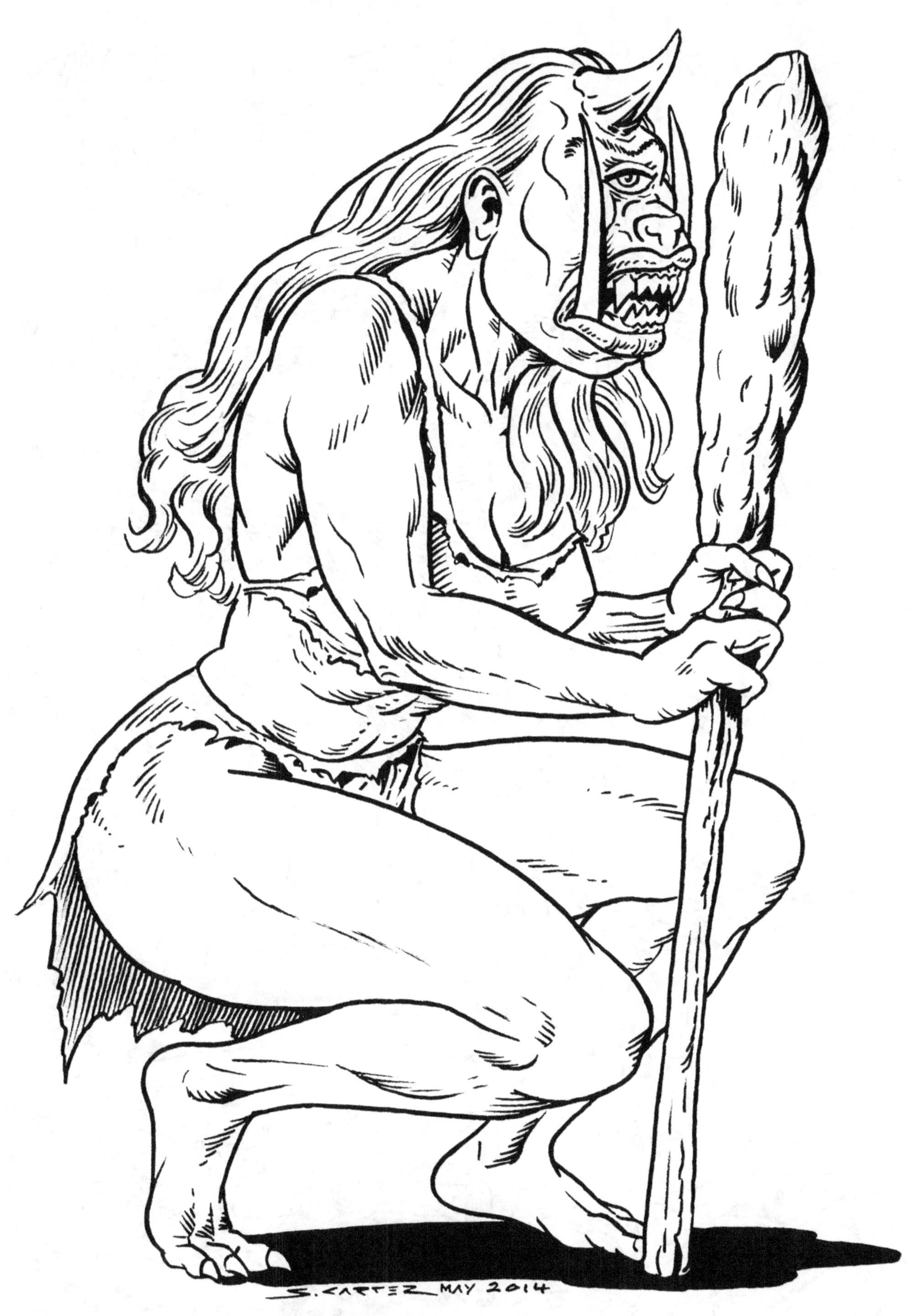

The Primal Man-Hunting Urp

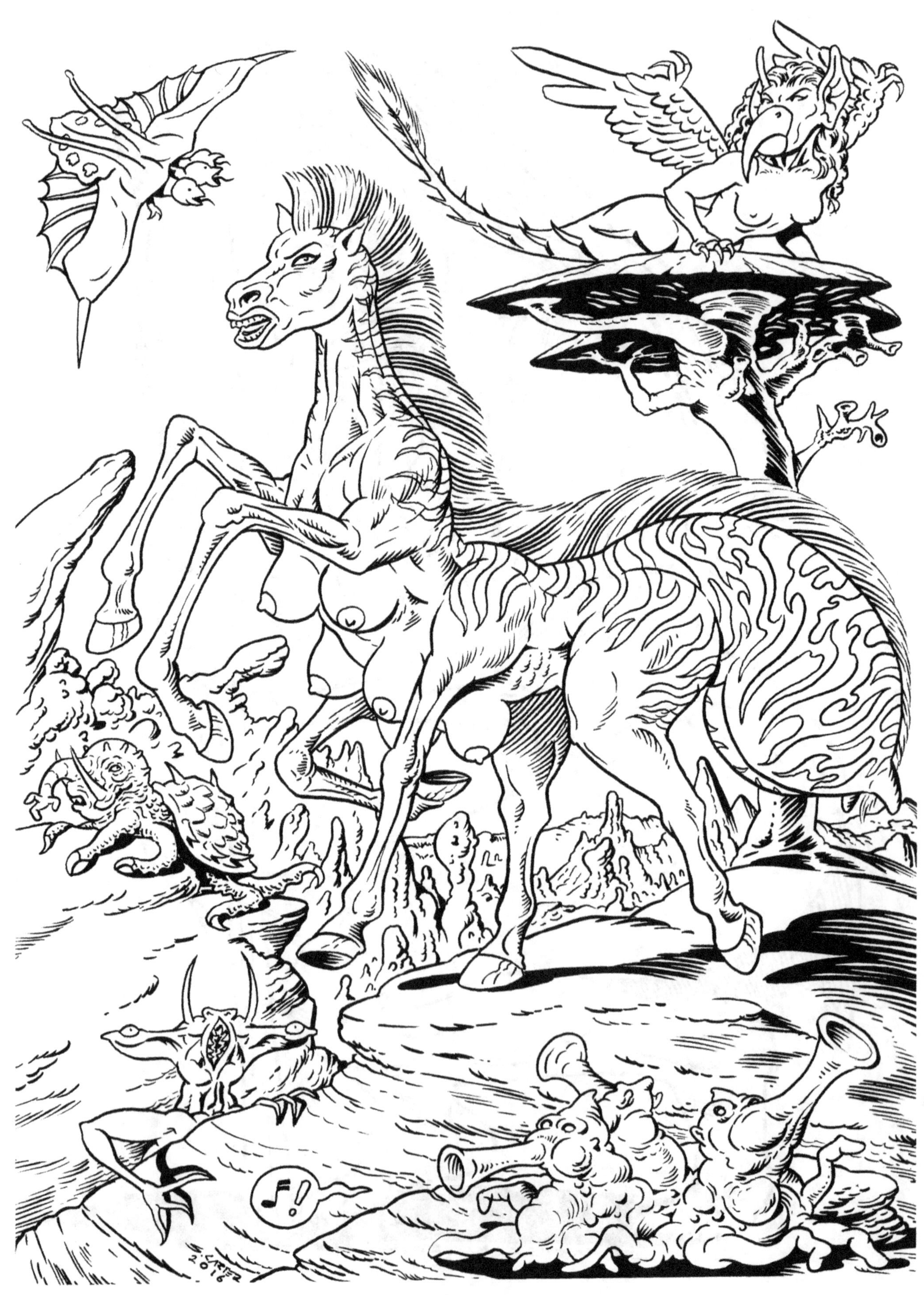

Preposterous Organic Anomalies

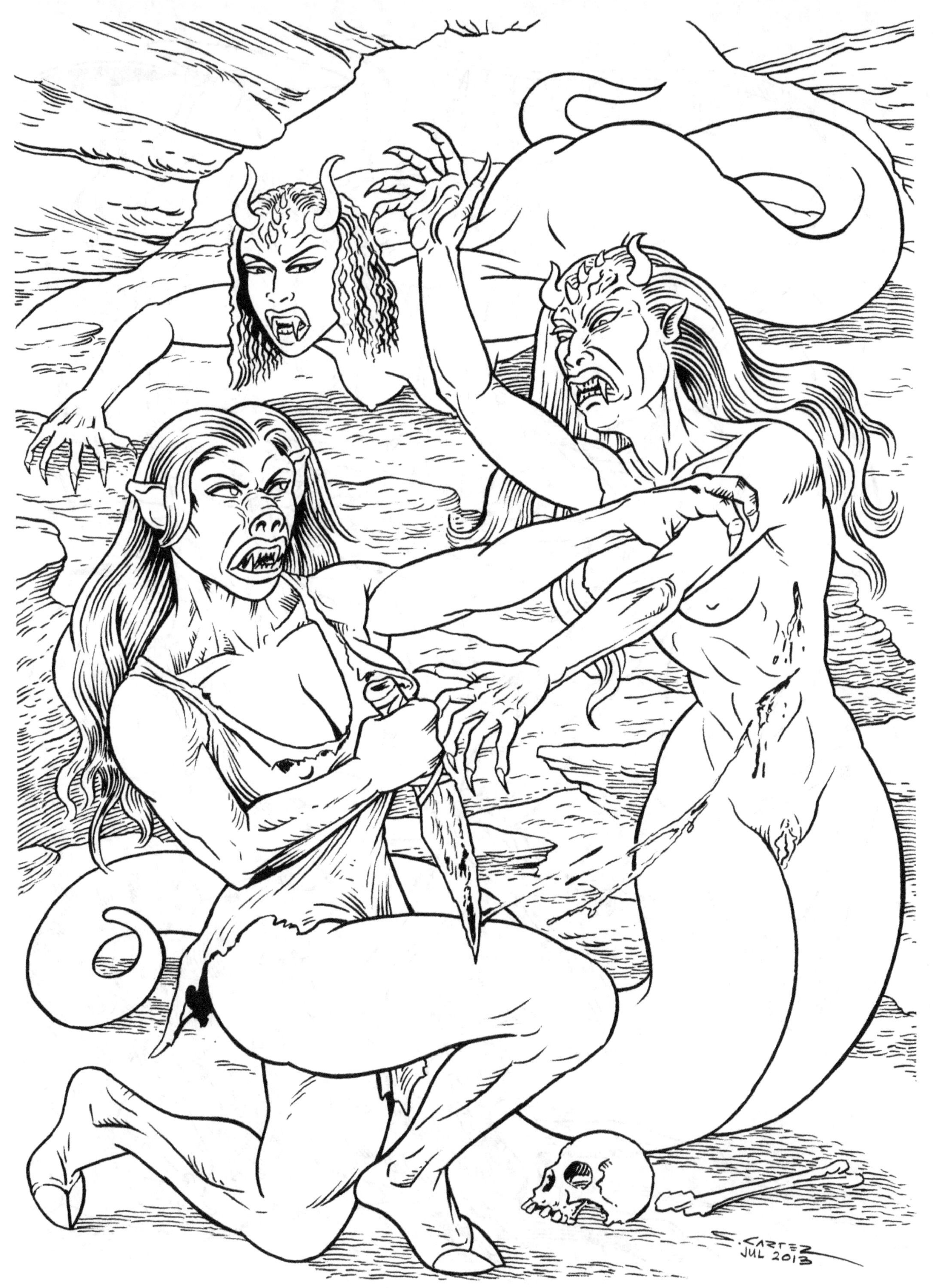

Den of Lamiae

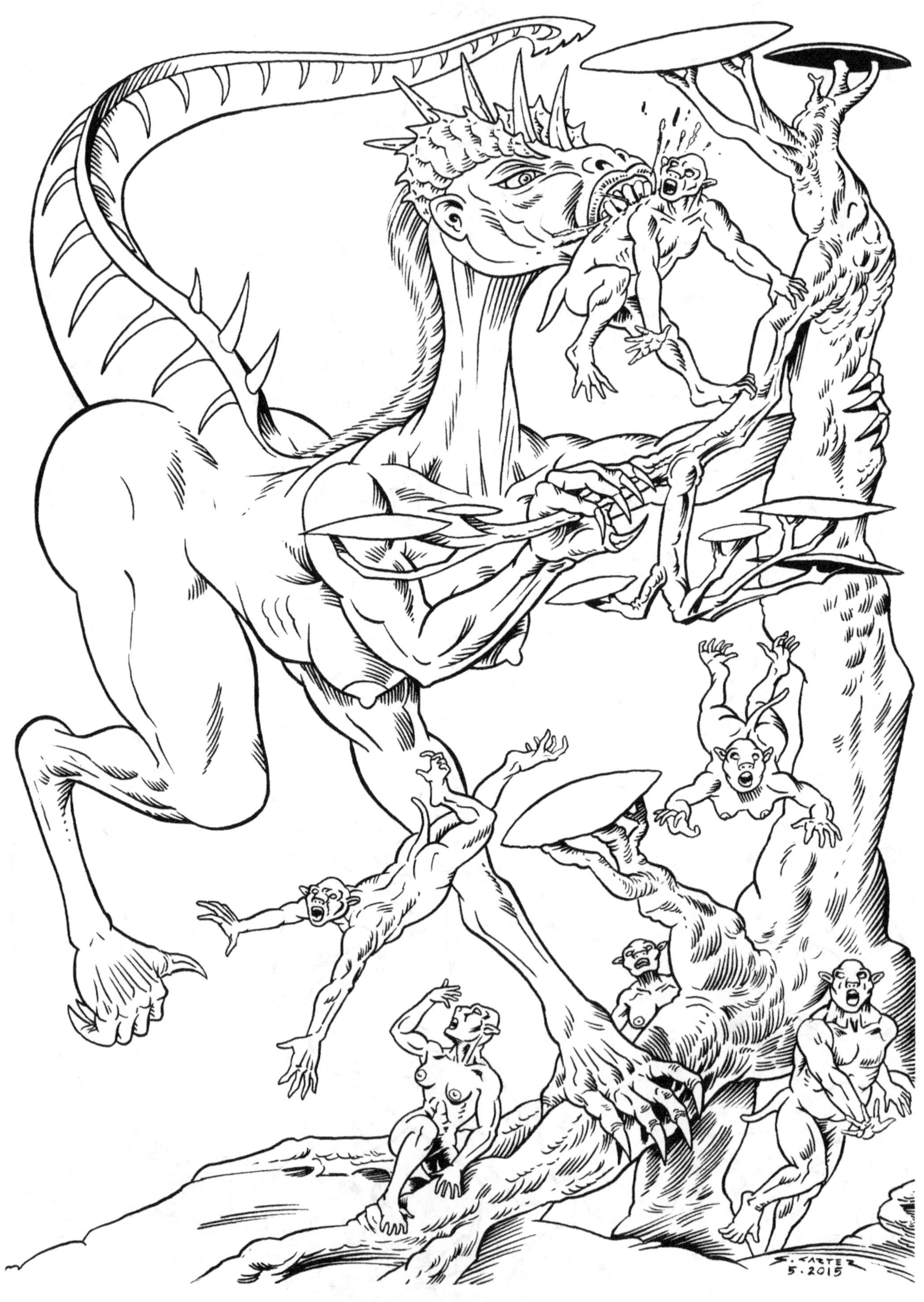

Carnofem Devouring Scurriers

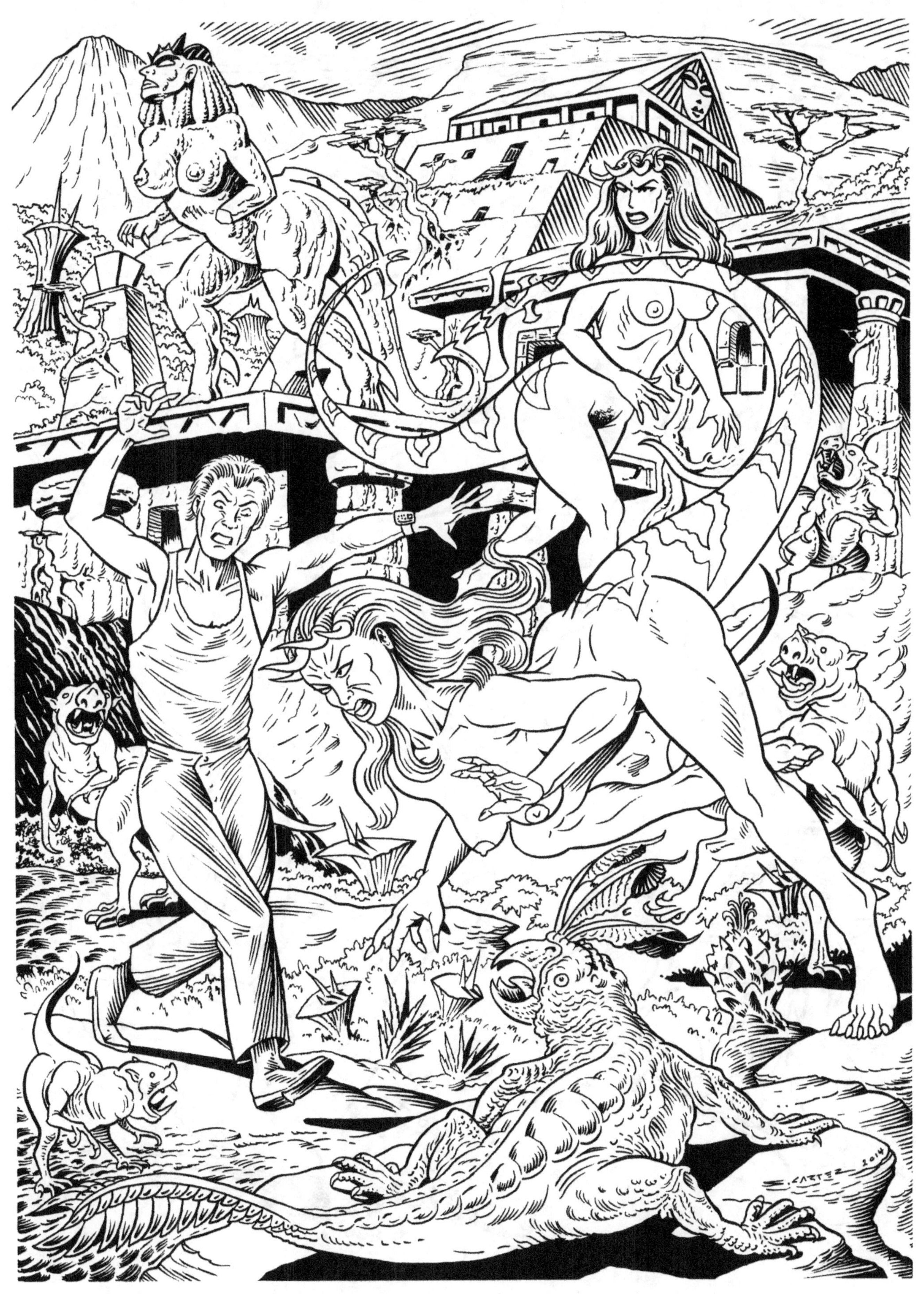

City of the Femosaur Goddess

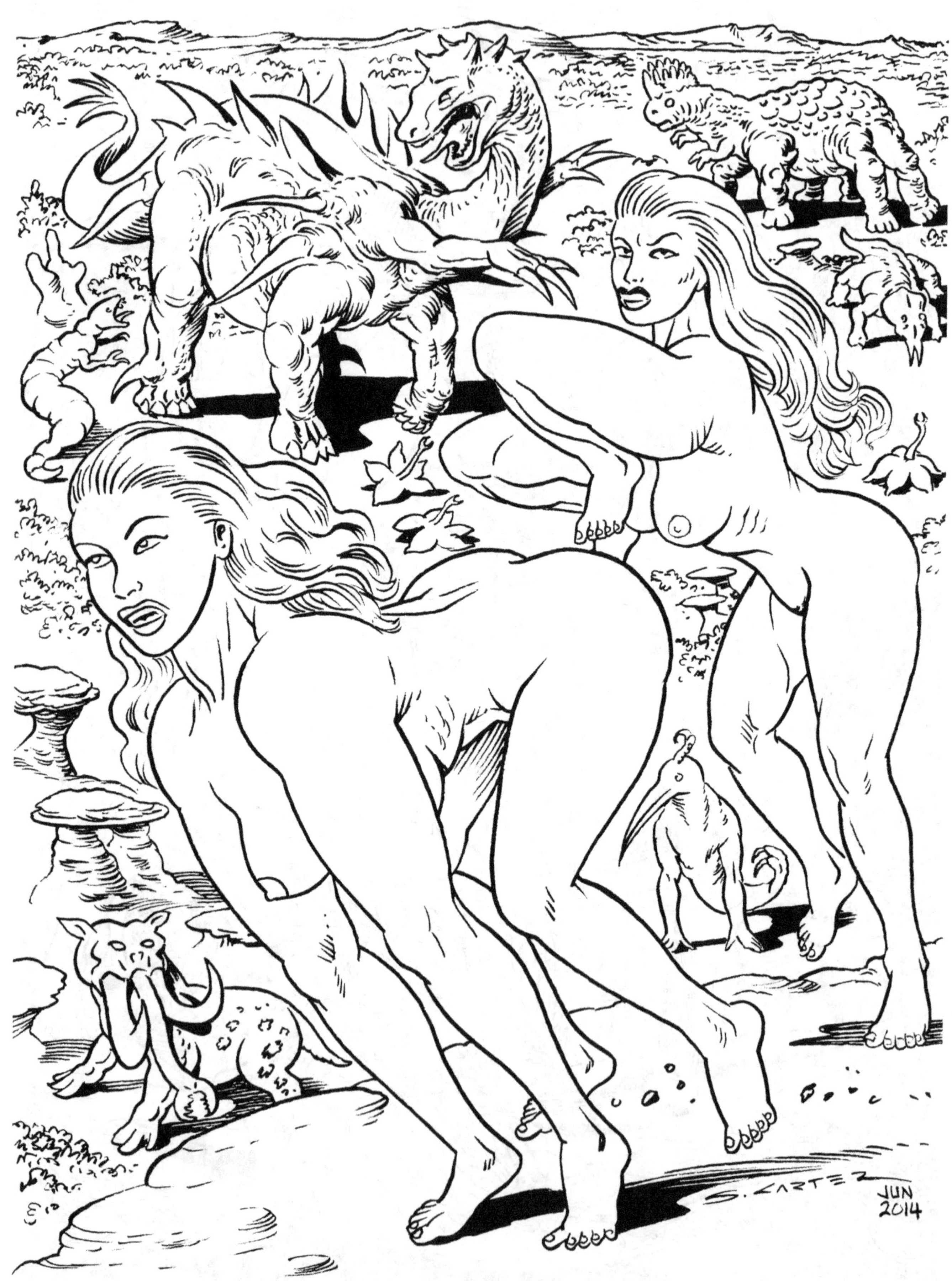

Two Femaquads

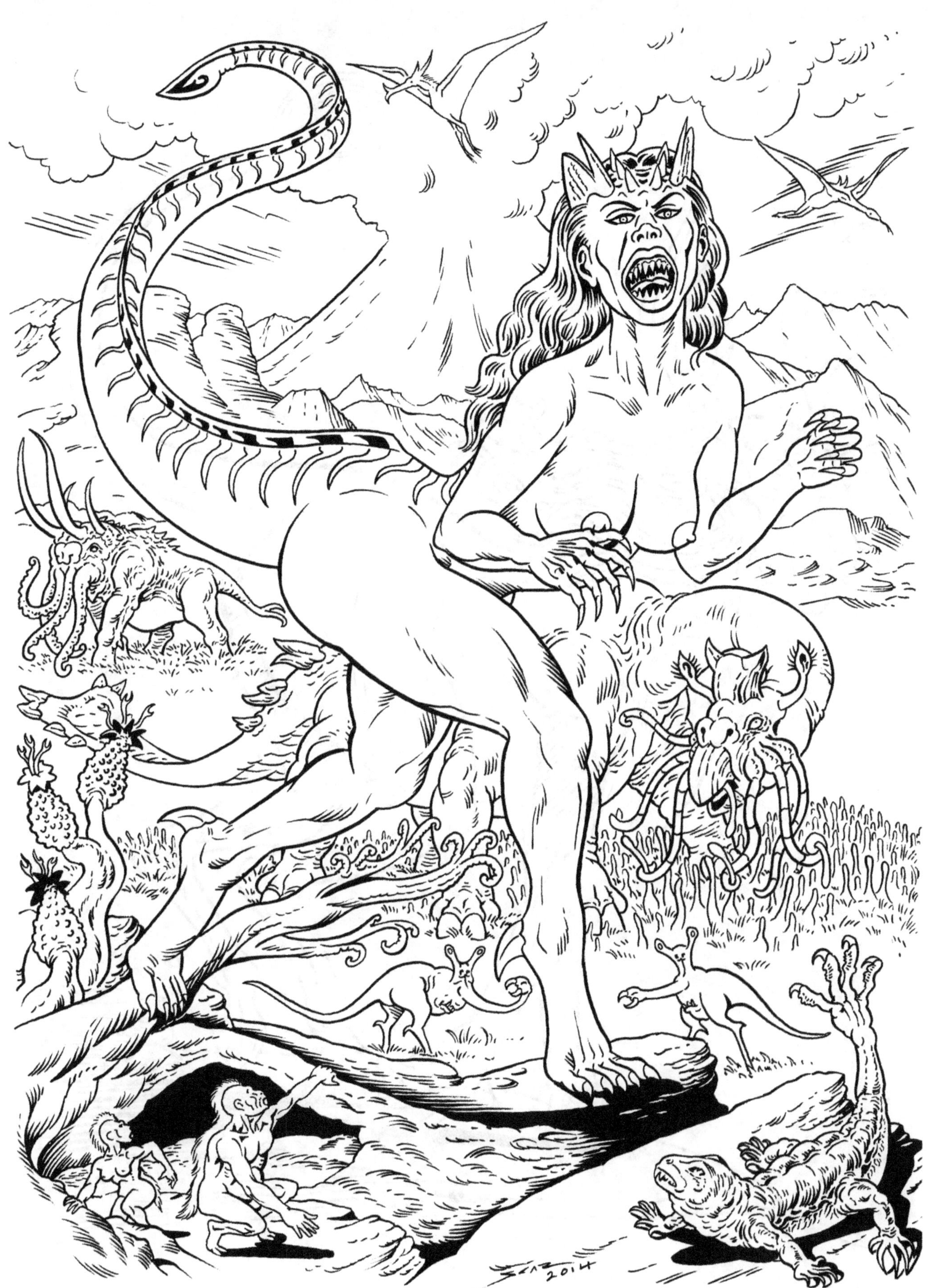

Deadly Debrosaur

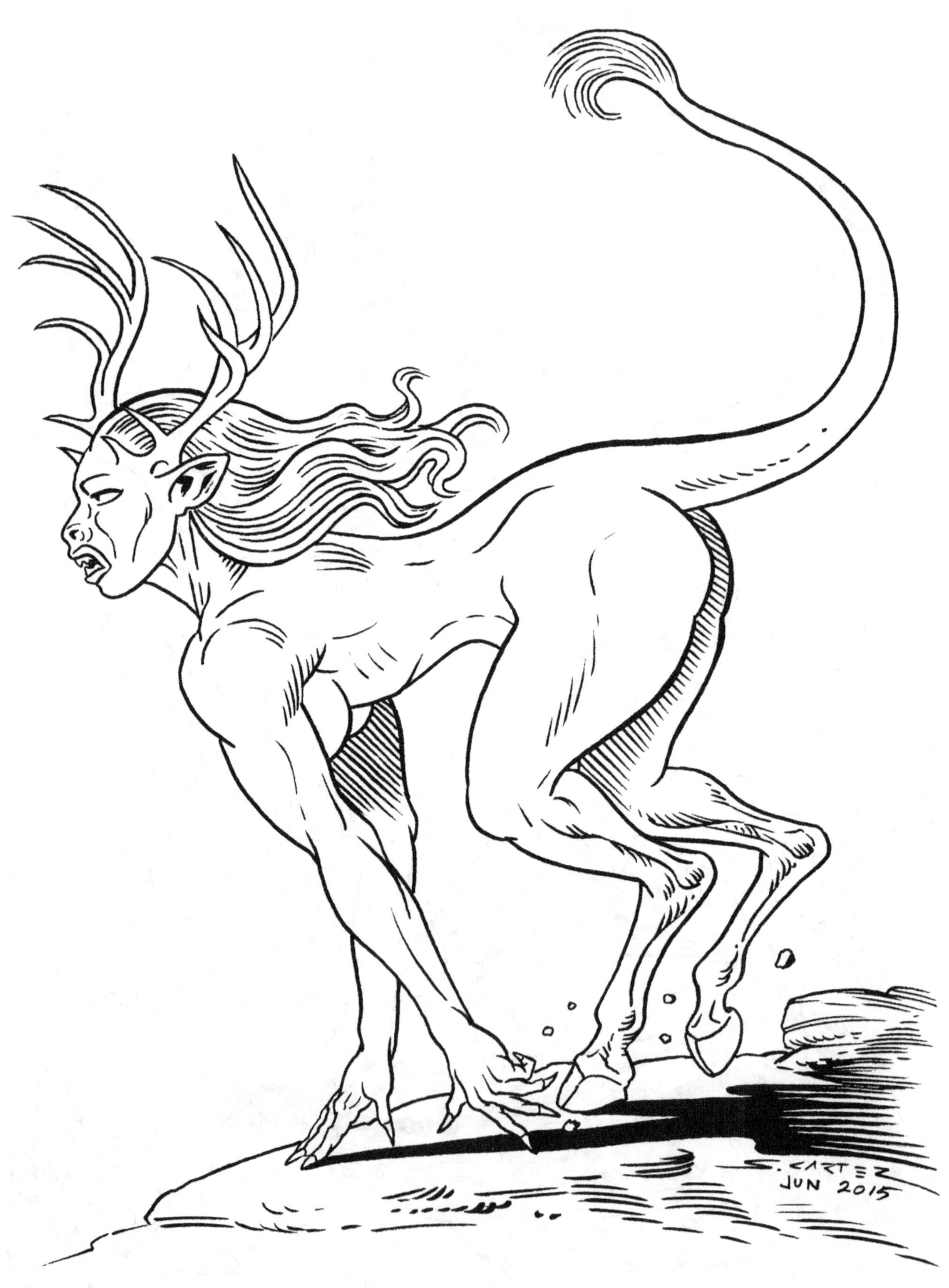

Wild Woodlands Trollop

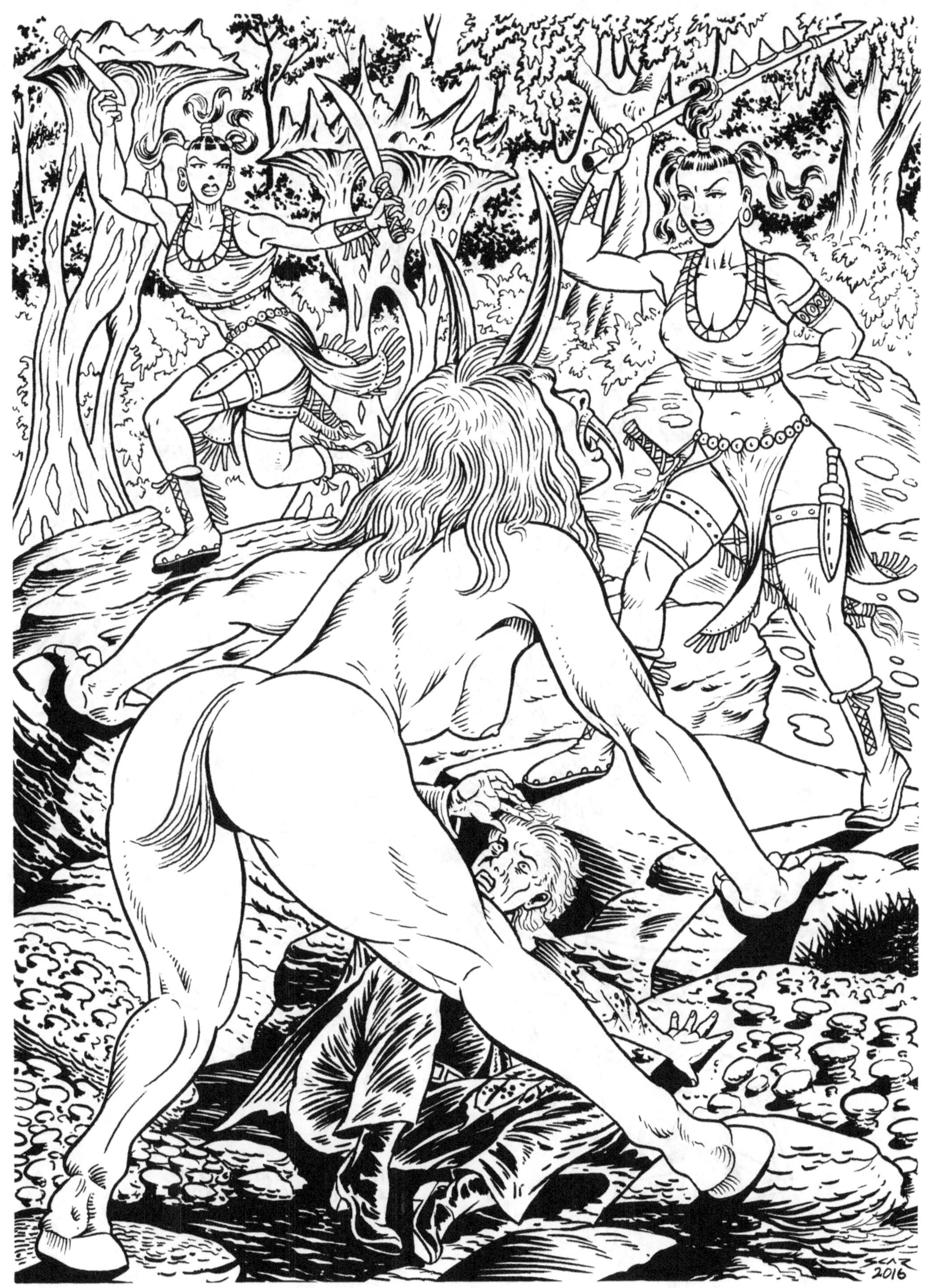

Earthman in Strife

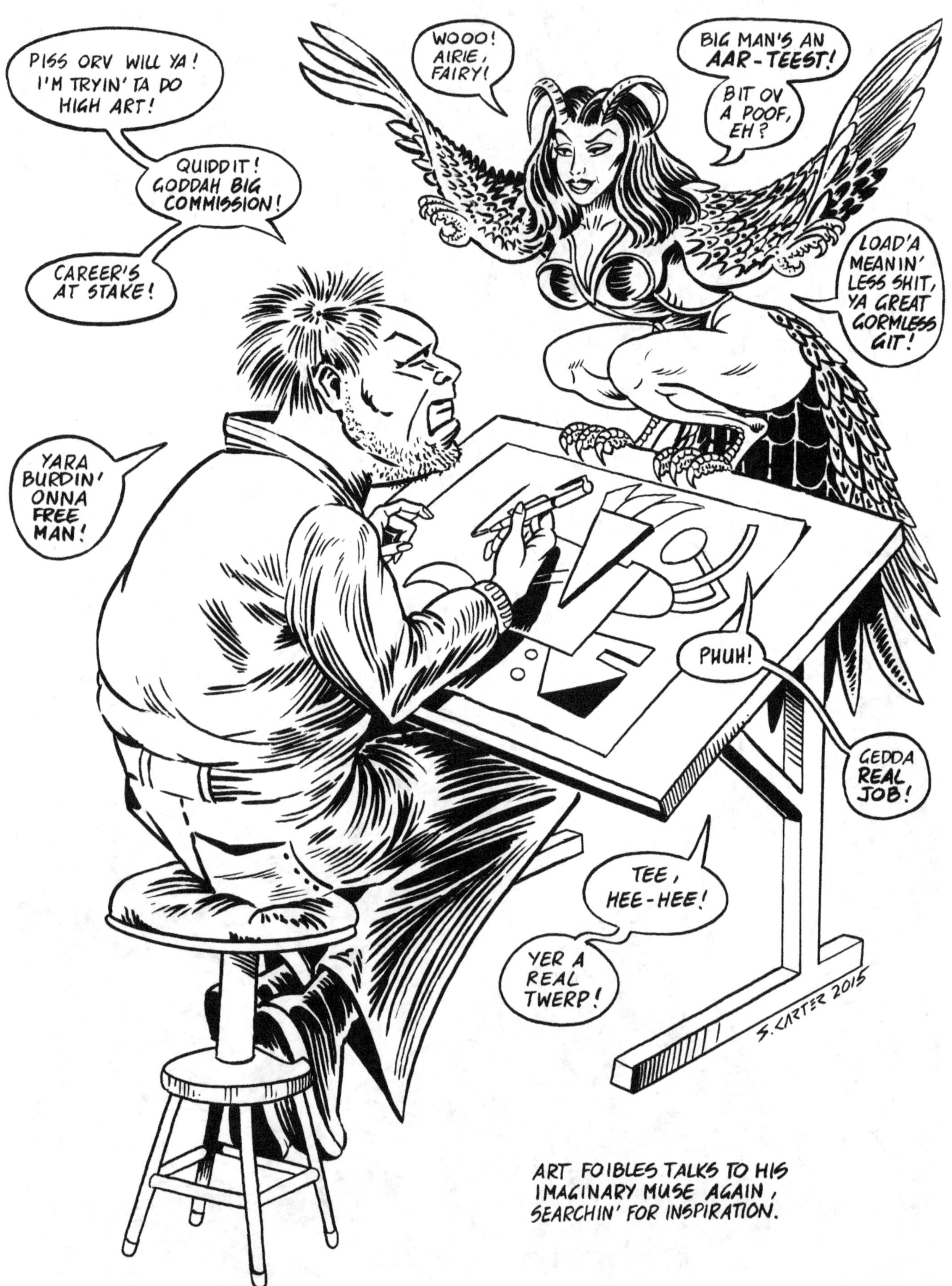

ART FOIBLES TALKS TO HIS IMAGINARY MUSE AGAIN, SEARCHIN' FOR INSPIRATION.

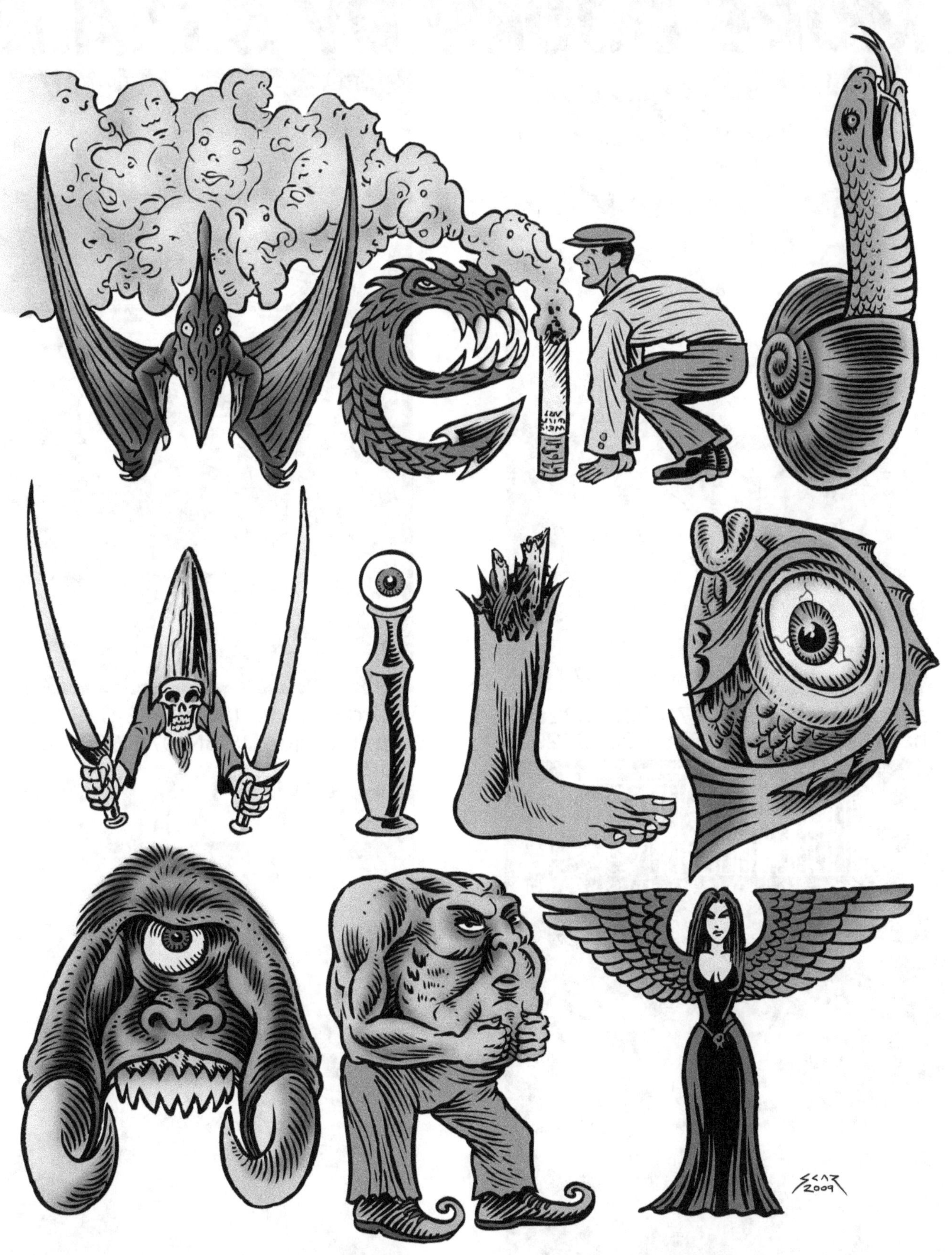

If you enjoyed this book by SCAR, have a look at their other titles and please consider writing a review. Thanks!

MORE BOOKS BY S.C.A.R.

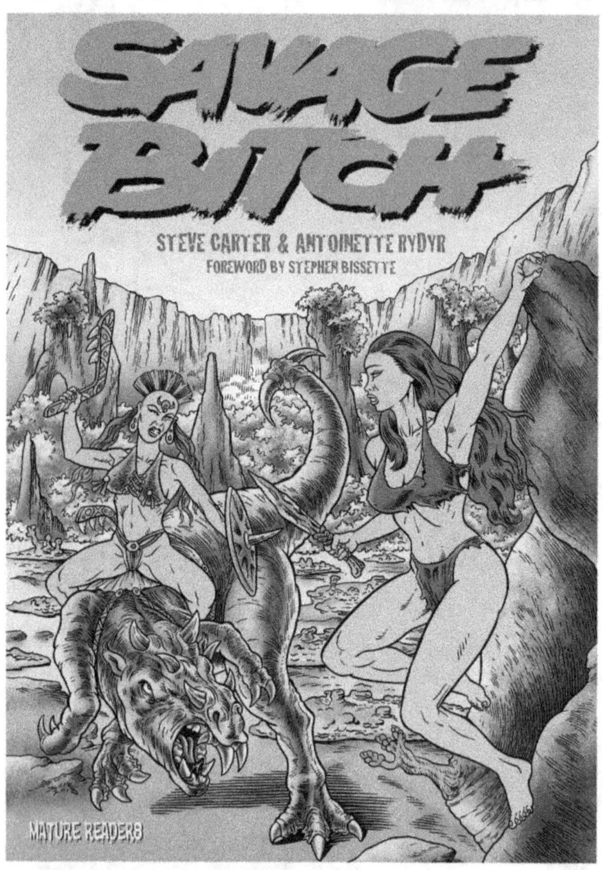

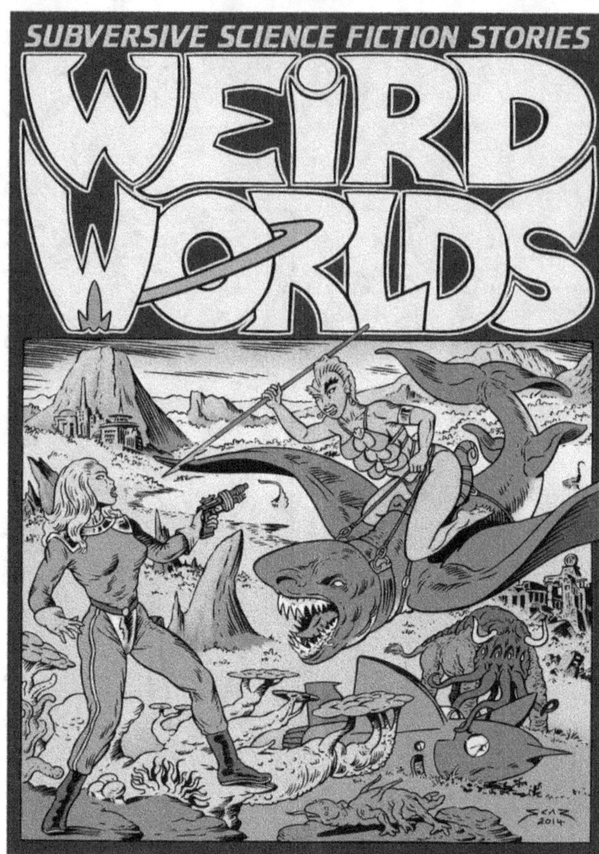

Savage Bitch: ISBN 978-0987622907
Phantastique: ISBN 978-0987622938

Weird Worlds: ISBN 978-0987622914
Fantastique: ISBN 978-0987622921

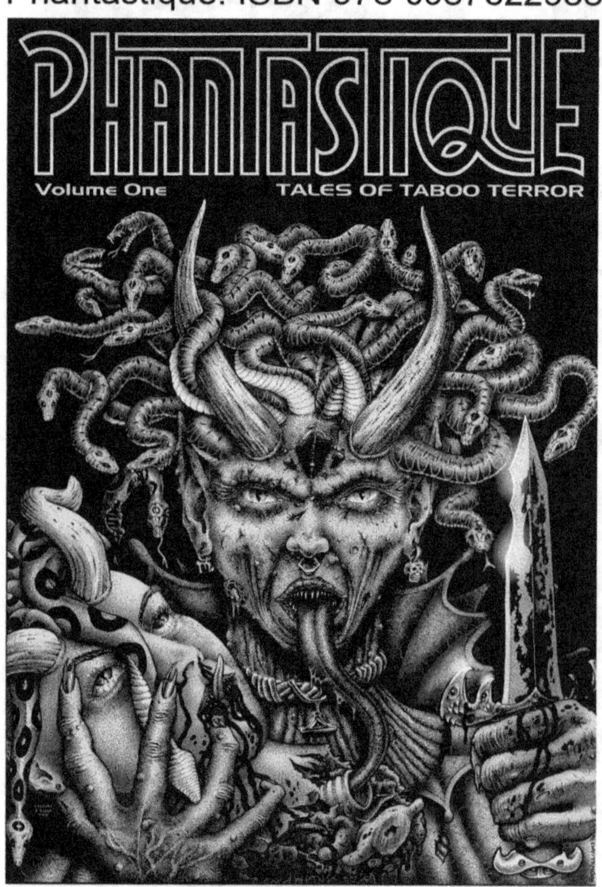

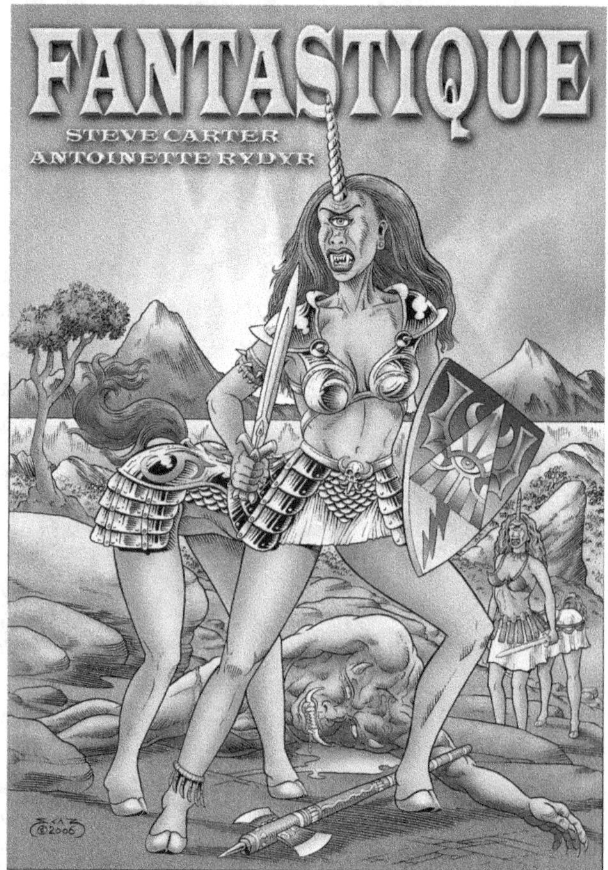

www.weirdwildart.com

MORE BOOKS BY S.C.A.R.

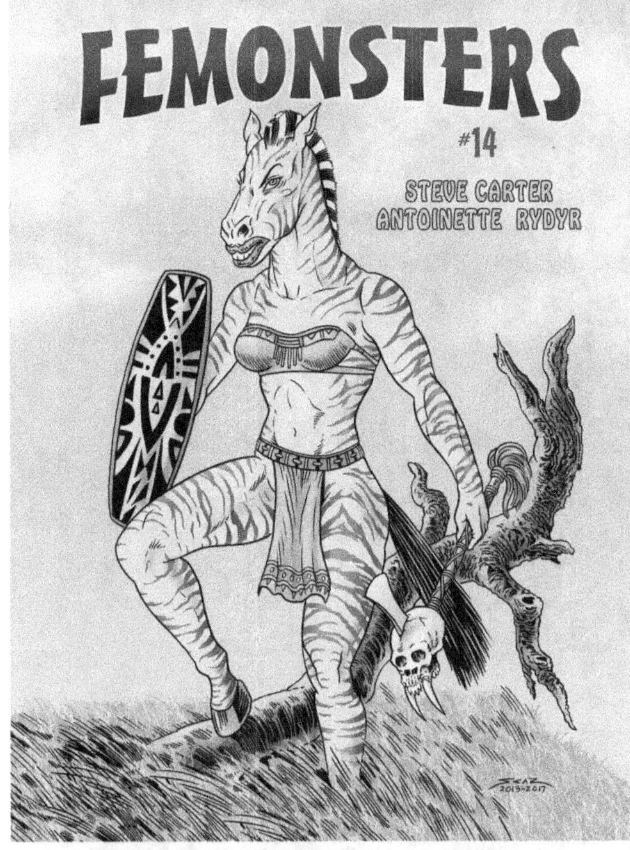

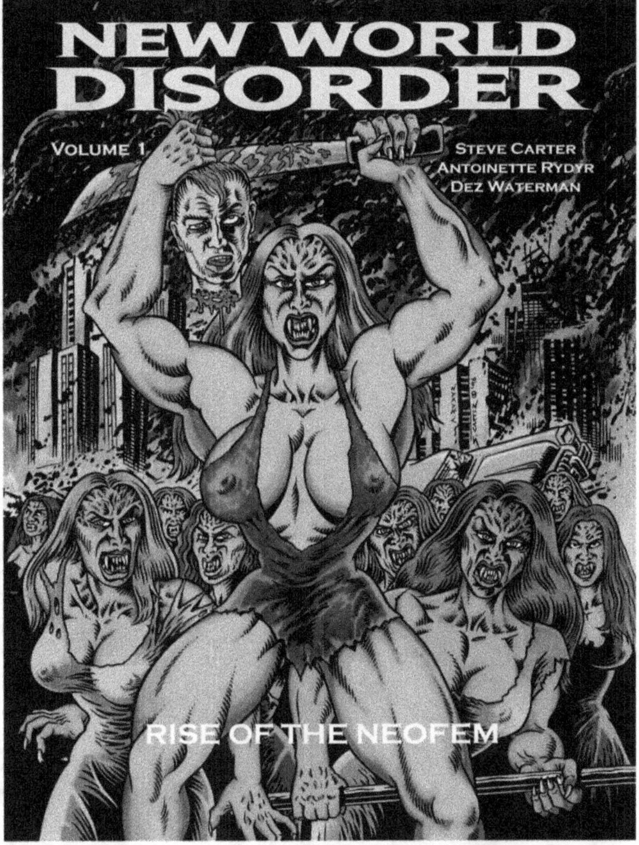

Femonsters #14: ISBN 978-0987622969
Bestiary of Monstruum: ISBN 978-0987622945

New World Disorder: ISBN 978-0987622976
Weird Sex Fantasy: ISBN 978-0987622952

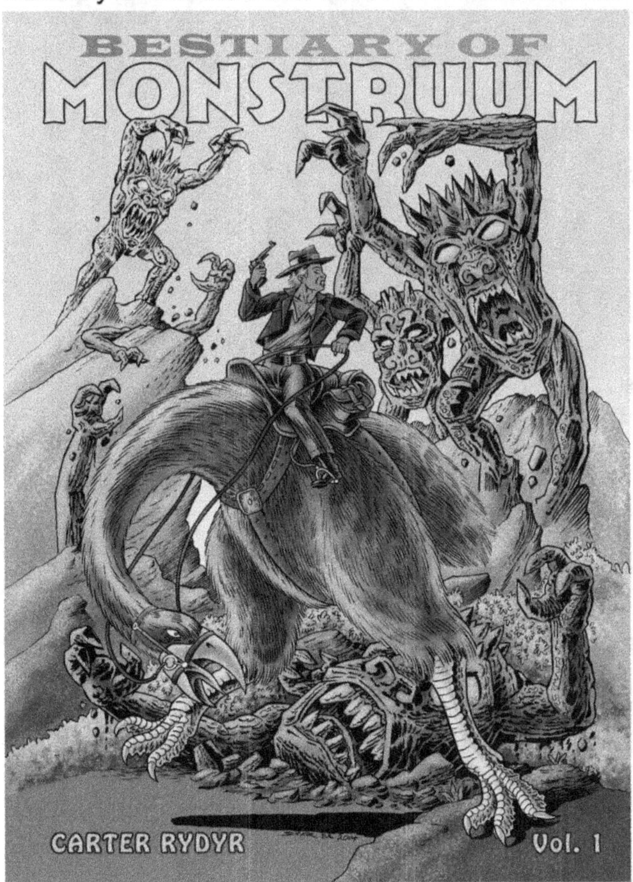

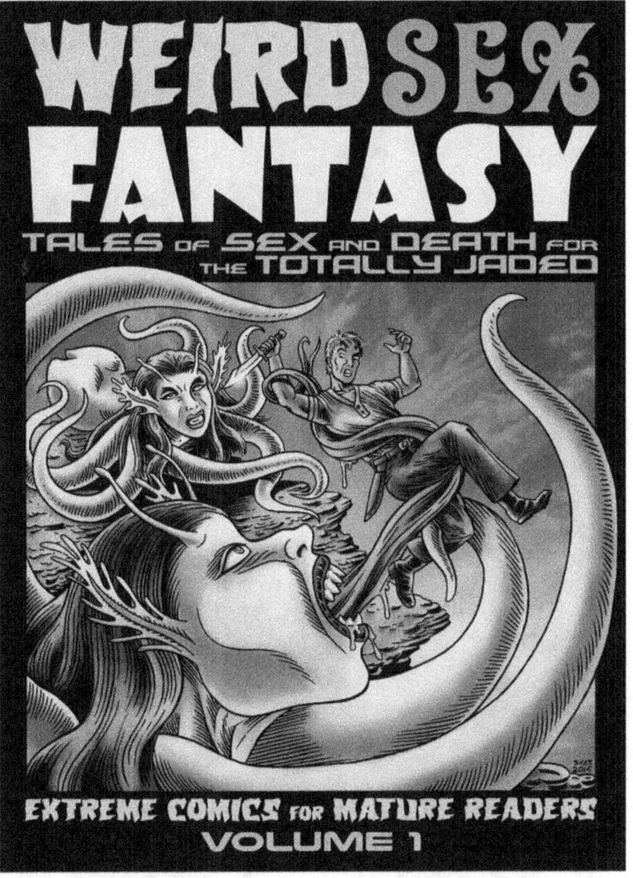

www.weirdwildart.com

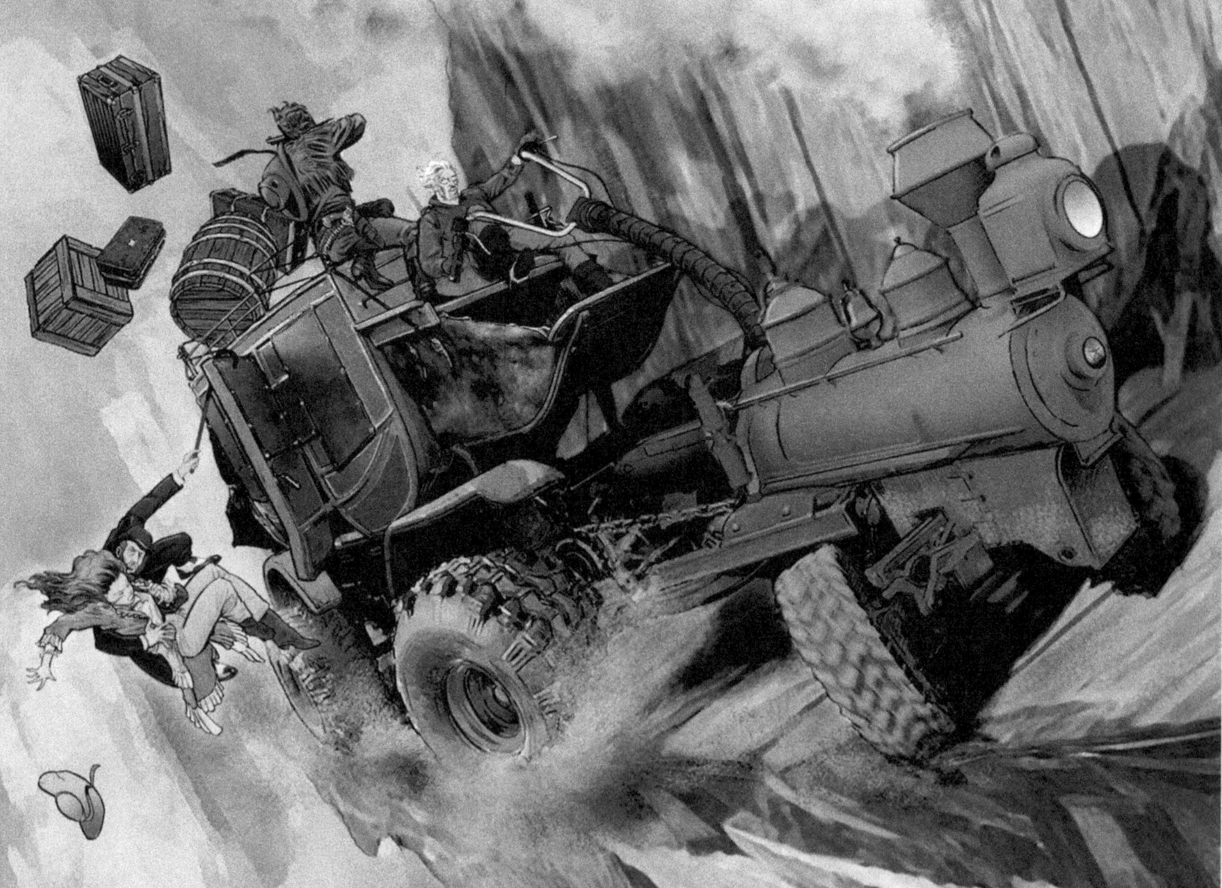
CARTER RYDYR AND ETHAN SOMERVILLE
WEIRD WILD WEST
PART 1 – HELL DORADO
PART 2 – THE GOOD, THE BAD AND THE ZOMBIE

WEIRD WILD WEST

A New Novel by
Carter Rydyr
Ethan Somerville

Imagine a wild west that isn't just full of cowboys and outlaws, saloon girls and gamblers. Imagine a wild west that isn't just cacti, tumbleweeds and rolling desert as far as the eye can see. Imagine a wild west of mechanical horses, mutant killer plants, flying dinosaurs, headless indians and fearsome zombie gunslingers hell-bent on revenge.

Imagine the Weird Wild West.

Six colourful characters, some not entirely human, embark on a perilous journey south from Sunbleached Plains to Kellyville. A dapper dentist, a southern belle, a wealthy madam, a retired banker turned gambler, an orphaned boy and a travelling body-parts salesman all trade their various stories to pass the time.

Driving the carriage is one Zeke "the Freak" Sarandon, a retired soldier with more than one strange, nervous habit. Although he is an experienced traveller, and the only one insane enough to take the most direct route south, even he cannot prevent his passengers from each meeting their grisly demise, one by one.

Hot on the trail of the coach, astride an ancient mechanical horse blowing sparks and belching out toxic clouds of smoke, is a zombie gunslinger, the risen corpse of a murdered prospector.

For on the carriage is the one who killed him, and he must have his horrible, bloody revenge.

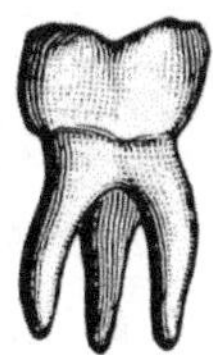

Bizarro Pulp Press
an imprint of JournalStone Publishing.

Published 2018

ISBN: 978-1-947654-40-2